Oh you four Winds that blow so strong

And know that this is true,

Stoop a little, and carry my song

To all the men I knew.

                (Kipling)

NARRATIVE

OF

Operations of Third Light Horse Brigade

(Including the Egyptian Rebellion 1919)

from

27th October, 1917

to

11th July, 1919

By
Brig. General L. C. WILSON
C.B., C.M.G., D.S.O., V.D., G.O.C. 3rd L. H. Brigade, A.I.F.

The Naval & Military Press Ltd

Published by
The Naval & Military Press Ltd
5 Riverside, Brambleside, Bellbrook
Industrial Estate, Uckfield, East Sussex,
TN22 1QQ England
Tel: +44 (0) 1825 749494
Fax: +44 (0) 1825 765701
www.naval-military-press.com
www.military-genealogy.com
www.militarymaproom.com

*In reprinting in facsimile from the original, any imperfections are inevitably reproduced
and the quality may fall short of modern type and cartographic standards.*

NARRATIVE

BY

BRIGADIER-GENERAL, L. C. WILSON, C.M.G., D.S.O.

OF

OPERATIONS OF THIRD LIGHT HORSE BRIGADE, A.I.F.

FROM

27th October 1917 to 4th March 1919.

APPENDICES.

A. Brigade Staff and Regimental Commanders.
B. The Sword.
C. Brigade Casualties.
D. Brigade evacuations for sickness.
E. Ration Scales.
F. Forage Scale.
G. Enemy Correspondence re Es-Salt Operations, May 1918.
H. Memo by Brigade Veterinary Officer.
J. Decorations awarded.

NARRATIVE OF OPERATIONS OF THE 3rd LIGHT HORSE B^de., AUSTRALIAN MOUNTED DIVISION

From 27th October 1917, to 4th March 1919.

Brigadier-General L. C. Wilson, C.M.G., D.S.O., Commanding.

With a view to understanding the references to other mounted troops in this narrative, the organisation of the mounted troops on the Palestine—Syria fronts, is set out as follows:—

The mounted troops on the above front, with the exception of a few squadrons, of Divisional Cavalry, etc., formed the Desert Mounted Corps, (Lieut.-General Sir H. G. Chauvel, K.C.B., K.C.M.G., Commanding). In the early part of the period covered by this narrative the Desert Mounted Corps consisted of 3 Divisions and the Imperial Camel Corps, viz:—(1). A. & .N. Z. Mounted Division, consisting of 1st and 2nd Light Horse Brigades, and N. Z. Mounted Rifle Brigade. (2). Australian Mounted Division consisting of 3rd and 4th Light Horse Brigades, and 5th Mounted Brigade, (Imperial Yeomanry), and (3). the Yeomanry Mounted Division, (3 Yeomanry Brigades). (4). The I.C.C. Brigade consisting of 3 A. & N. Z. Battalions and 1 Imperial Battalion. In the middle of 1918 the Desert Mounted Corps was reorganised, certain of the Yeomanry Regiments were sent to Europe as machine gunners, and 12 Indian Cavalry Regiments were brought to this front. The I.C.C. Brigade was broken up and the 5th Light Horse Brigade, (2 Regiments), was formed from the Australian personnel and this new Brigade went in to the Australian Mounted Division in lieu of the 5th Mounted Brigade, (Yeomanry). Therefore, in the September and October 1918 operations the Corps consisted of 4 Divisions, namely:—The A. & N. Z. Mounted Division, the Australian Mounted Division, the 4th Cavalry Division and the 5th Cavalry Division, each of these two last mentioned Divisions were one-third British Yeomanry and two thirds Indian Cavalry. As the 5th Light Horse Brigade had only 2 Regiments, during the final operations of September and October the French Regiment of Mixed Cavalry was attached to that Brigade for those operations.

The 3rd Light Horse Brigade as above stated forms part of the Australian Mounted Division (Major-General. W. H. Hodgson, C.V.O,, C.B., Commanding). The Brigade consists of the following Units:—Brigade Headquarters, 8th, 9th and 10th Light Horse Regiments, 3rd Australian Machine Gun Squadron, 3rd Signal Troop, 3rd Light Horse Field Ambulance, and the 8th Mobile Veterinary Section—Total establishment varied from slightly over 2,000 to slightly under that number. In addition to the above Units there were usually attached a troop of the Australian Engineers and a battery of British Royal Horse Artillery. (The Notts Battery, 4 guns, 13 or 18 pounders). After the second battle of Gaza, April 1917, the Turkish Army occupied a line from the coast at Gaza to Beersheba. The British line ran from the coast at Gaza to Gamli, about 4 mile south of Shelal, on the Wadi Ghuzzee. On our right flank there was, therfeore, a distance of about 15 miles between our entrenched line and the enemy entrenched line at Beersheba. For the 6 months prior to the big offensive in the end of October, 1917, this country was patrolled and reconnoitred by the Desert Mounted Corps. One division held a line on the Wadi Ghuzzee, Shellal—Gamli, and watched the right flank westerly to Ghabi, the second division was bivouaced in support at Abasan El Kebir, and the third division was in reserve on the beach near Khan Yunus. The front line division usually held the position for about a month and then went into reserve. This Brigade took it's tour of duty of patrol and reconnaissance work. This work was not uninteresting. The country is open and undulating with no obstacles to Cavalry. The Turks sent out their cavalry patrols daily, sometimes they would support them with infantry and guns,

On numerous occasions the opposing horsemen met, but unless the enemy came out in overwhelming numbers, as they did on a few occasions, they would never stand up to our mounted troops. Many were the ambushes laid for their patrols, some of which were successful, others were not, as the Turk was very careful about getting into trouble. Small parties of our men were left out at nights in huts and gullies, their horses being sent miles back to cover. On other occasions the Mounted troops, including this Brigade, formed strong covering parties to enable General Officers, Artillery Officers, and Survey Officers to reconnoitre the country to within range of the enemy guns on their Beersheba positions. Raids were also made on their advanced works near Beersheba and Irgeig. A raid was made upon their railway at Asluj, where every rail in 17 miles of line was destroyed with gun cotton. In September and October these reconnaissances, particularly, those towards the south and south west of Beersheba, were more frequently carried out.

The Command-in-Chief decided to attack the Turkish centre at Sheria, first obtaining possession of Beersheba. The necessary steps were taken to cause the enemy to believe that the main attack would be at Gaza. Documents since captured from the enemy have proved that the enemy were deceived as to General Allenby's intention. October 31st was appointed the day for the attack on Beersheba, ("Z" day). The preliminary operations for this offensive began on the 20th October. Shortly after that date the 2nd Light Horse Brigade proceeded to Asluj, 17 miles south of Beersheba to develop water. It was the intention of the Commander-in-Chief that the Desert Mounted Corps should march round the south of Beersheba, and attack that place from the east and north east, while the infantry should attack it from the west.

On 27th October Lieut. Col. L. C. Wilson, C.M.G., then commanding the 5th Light Horse Regiment, was appointed to command this Brigade. The Brigade had been for some time prior to this, commanded temporarily by Lieut. Col. L. C. Maygar, V.C., D.S.O., during the absence on leave of Brigadier-General Royston, C.M.G., D.S.O. This last mentioned Officer decided not to return to Egypt.

On 27th October the Turkish force at Beersheba, no doubt, noticing signs of activity on this flank, pushed out a strong reconnaissance. At 0830 on this morning, this Brigade was ordered out to support the 8th Mounted Brigade, who were being heavily attacked by enemy infantry and cavalry on the outpost line, point 720—630 and 550, (Ref. Map Beersheba 1/125.000). The Brigade passed clear of the wire entanglements on the east of Wadi Ghuzzee at 0945. The 10th Light Horse Regiment was despatched at the trot to move on El Buggar from the south. On arrival of the remainder of Brigade at the command post of the 8th Mounted Brigade, that Unit reported that the enemy had surrounded the position at point 630 and 550, but that one squadron was still holding out on point 720. The 9th Regiment, with 2 machine guns, moved at once to support the squadron on point 720. Shortly afterwards the Turks surrounded the Yeomanry on point 720 and captured the position—the garrison behind annihilated. At 1530 the 9th Light Horse Regiment was under instructions to counter attack point 720 but a patrol of that Regiment occupied it at 1600. Orders were received that the infantry, would take over under cover of darkness. This taking over was completed at 2300 and the Brigade returned to Bivouac at 0400 on 28th. Orders were now received for the concentration of the Australian and New Zealand Mounted Division and the Australian Mounted Division at Asluj, on the night of the 30th, with a view to those two Divisions being to the east of Beersheba on the morning of the 31st October.

All ranks had been given to understand that the success of the Commander-in-Chief's plans would depend to a considerable extent on the achievements of the mounted troops, at the initial stages in the flanking and enveloping movement set them. A thorough preparation had been made.

At 1500 on the 28th October, all transport of the Brigade was formed up at Um Urgan, in column of route, ready to join up with remainder of Divisional Transport, at Fara, and proceed to Esani—a march of 11 miles.

It may be here remarked that the Brigade and Regimental Transport is for the purpose of ease in handling divided into three categories, viz:—

A. *Echelon*—consisting of water carts and limbered wagons carrying reserve ammunition, signalling gear, (such as telephones), oil for motor cycles, etc. *Note* This transport always goes with the fighting troops, if it is possible for wheels to go over the ground.

B1. Echelon. Carries one day's rations for men and one day's fodder for horses.

B2. Echelon. Carries Cook's gear and necessary baggage.

Note. This transport is left behind on the slightest provocation.

Rations are either ordinary, mobile special emergency or iron, fodder is ordinary, mobile or special emergency. Full particulars are set out in appendexis " E " and " F " hereto.

8th Light Horse Regiment and 3 sub-sections, (6 guns), M.G.S., had been detailed as escort to Divisional wheeled transport, and at 1700, the Divisional column, (307 vehicles), moved from Tel El Fara to Esani.

At 1500 the Brigade, less 8th Light Horse Regiment and 6 guns, of 3rd M.G.S. moved from bivouac at Um Urgan in column of route, and at 1730 passed the Divisional starting point, 2 miles south east of Tel El Fara, forming column of squadrons in line of troop column, and following in rear of 4th Brigade.

By 2245 the Brigade, less transport, was in bivouac at Esani, and by 2330, the rear of transport column had arrived at Esani. B squadron, 8th Light Horse Regiment, and 2 machine guns continued the march on to Khalasa, as escort to Divisional Troops and Divisional wheeled transport. The march was a severe one for transport animals. The track was heavy.

Oct. 29.

At 1700 the Brigade moved to Khalasa, (8 miles), in column of route, crossing Wadi Maalaga at a point 1½ miles south of Esani. Khalasa reached at 2130 and horses watered at Khalasa wells, which had been blown in by the Turks and partly repaired by our Engineers, assisted by the Camel Brigade.

Horses and men were marching well, although the dusty conditions along the line of march were becoming very stifling. Transport difficulties were increasing on account of the state of the track caused by the traffic of the Anzac Mounted Division, which had proceeded the Australian Mounted Division. The original track, earth and sand, was in an extremely soft condition on account of the absence of rain for many months previously.

Oct. 30.

8th Light Horse Regiment and 1 sub-section, M.G.S., were detailed to march to Asluj, reporting to General Staff, Anzac Mounted Division, by 0500 in 30th October. They moved from Khalasa at 0130 on 30th.

Between 0900 and 1000 a hostile aeroplane flew over Khalasa and was engaged by our own aircraft. Enemy plane was driven down. Thus, information of the movement of our mounted troops was not received by the enemy, and the attack on Beersheba from the east on the following morning was a great surprise to him.

At 1700 the Brigade, less 8th Light Horse Regiment, and 1 sub-section 3rd M.G.S. was formed up, in column of route, and joined in rear of Divisional Headquarters as the Australian Mounted Division moved forward. 10th L.H. under Lieut. Colonel T. J. Todd, D.S.O., with one sub-section M.G.S. formed the advanced guard to the Divisional column.

" A " echelon transport travelled in rear of it's own Brigade group. B1 and B2 echelon remained at Khalasa until daylight, 31st October, and then travelled forward under orders of A.A. & Q.M.G., Division.

Asluj was reached at 2200, but owing to small water supply the column was delayed near 2 hours. Draught animals only were watered, the supply would not allow of more. There had been several large wells at Asluj furnishing a good supply of water. These wells were some 70 feet deep. The wells, had, however, lately been blown in by the Turks. The 2nd Brigade had during the preceding week been engaged in day and night shifts clearing them out. The original flow, however, was not forthcoming and the supply was not up to expectations or requirements.

At 2400 the Brigade moved Asluj for the point of Divisional concentration Iswaiwan—a march of 31 miles. Heavy rains had fallen over the area two days previously and guns and transport met with difficulties when crossing the Wadi Imshash. On the other hand the stifling dust trouble was not experienced. Its absence gave great relief to the troops and animals, and allowed them to arrive at the point of concentration ready for action in a fitter condition, than had rising dust been experienced.

The march from Asluj to Iswaiwan was in many places over stoney country. The track was only in fair order due to the traffic of the Anzac Mounted Division ahead.

Notwithstanding that the march had been continuous, except for 2 hours at Asluj, since 1700 on the previous afternoon, when daylight broke, men were not showing signs of fatigue, although many of the riding horses were evidently in want of water.

Oct. 31.

Shortly after 0530 our advanced troops gained touch with the Anzac Mounted Division in the vicinity of Iswaiwan. Here water in shallow pools was discovered and many of the horses were given a short drink, although time would not permit of all horses being watered.

The Australian Mounted Division shortly afterwards concentrated. Final orders for the Division were to be received at the point of concentration. The Division would be called upon for either one or two tasks by the Desert Mounted Corps, whose double mission was,

(a). To attack Beersheba, from the east, and envelope the enemy's left rear, and

(b). To sieze as much water supply as possible in order to form a base for future operations. The 20th Corps would co-operate with Desert Mounted Corps by attacking Beersheba defences from the west and south west. The capture of Beersheba being the primary object of the army.

The Australian Mounted Division was to be prepared at Iswaiwan for a quick move either north westward on Beersheba or northwards to assist Anzac Mounted Division, who were moving to attack Tel El Saba.

From the rear of the Anzac Mounted Division, 8th Light Horse Regiment, under Lieut. Colonel L. C. Maygar, V.C., D.S.O., was detached at 0630 to take up the line 1280—1180—1210, and get into signalling communication with 7th Mounted Brigade, (operating on right of 20th Corps), on the left, and N.Z.M.R. Brigade, (operating on the left of Anzac Mounted Division), on the right.

8th Light Horse Regiment was linked up with right and left by 0800. Enemys positions and works at Ras Ghannam, were reconnoitred vigorously and discovered to be very strongly held.

After receipt of reports of the patrols, who had been reconnoitring enemy's positions E.S.E., S. and S.W. of Beersheba, during the morning, orders were received that the main attack would be launched against the enemy's position at Tel El Saba.

The Anzac Mounted Division were pushing the attack now on the right, and at 1400 the Brigade (less 8th L.H. Regiment) received orders to move to assist the Anzac Mounted Division at Tel El Saba, being temporarily attached to that Division for this purpose.

On moving across open country immediately towards Bir Salim Abu Irgeig, the Brigade came under heavy shell fire. The formation of the Brigade in this movement was squadron column in line of troop column, with double interval and distance.

On the arrival of the Brigade at the point of deployment Bir Salim Abu Irgeig, at 1500, the 9th Light Horse Regiment under Lieut. Colonel W. H. Scott, D.S.O., was ordered into the attack on the right of the N.Z.M.R. Brigade, supported by the rest of the Brigade, less the 8th Regiment. The 9th Light Horse Regiment moved forward across the open ground to the north of the main wadi where it came under intense enemy shelling, but suffered very few casualties. The movement was carried out with the Regiment in column of squadrons, each squadron in line of troop column, with 100 yards interval and distance between troops. The determination with which the movement was executed undoubtedly had a moral effect on the enemy, who was now being closed in on. The balance of the Brigade moved in support along the bed of the main wadi.

The enemy's position at Tel El Saba was at 1530 captured with the garrison by the N.Z.M.R. Brigade before the 9th Regiment dismounted for action.

The 10th Light Horse Regiment at 1630 was ordered to seize the positions 1020 and 970, and cut off any enemy retreat along the Beersheba—Hebron road.

The 9th L.H. Regiment was now ordered to move from 1080 to Tel El Saba, and take up a second line 1040—960, to co-operate with the 10th L.H. Regiment holding the line 1020—970, in cutting off an enemys retreat (from Beersheba towards) Hebron.

When nearing Tel El Saba the 9th L.H. Regiment was bombed by 2 enemy aeroplanes flying at the extremely low altitudes of 800 feet, and suffered very heavy casualties in both men and horses. Including the sub-section M.G.S. attached to 9th L.G. Regiment, casualties sustained were:—13 other ranks killed, and 3 Officers and 17 other ranks wounded, 26 horses wounded and 32 horses killed.

The 8th L.H. Regiment had received orders from Headquarters, Anzac Mounted Division to rejoin 3rd Brigade Headquarters. When so doing they were also bombed by enemy aircraft flying at a very low altitude. The C.O. Lieut Col. Maygar, V.C., D.S.O., was here mortally wounded, and died the following day.

At about 1900 news was received that Beersheba had been captured. The enemy had been taken by surprise, they had not expected a serious attack on this flank. Information of the movement in force of the Mounted Troops towards Asluj was not gained by the enemy. The enemy aeroplane which did detect the movement of troops to the south failed to return.

The 10th Light Horse Regiment was meeting strong opposition from an enemy rearguard, who advanced against one squadron, and entrenched themselves in front of the 10th Light Horse position. The opening up of machine gun and rifle fire at about 2130 drove the enemy back. 10th Light Horse Regiment advanced troops had now entered Beersheba from the N.E. All Regiments and the machine gun squadron of the Brigade had during the day taken part in the attack. The casualties in the Brigade incurred for the day's operations were 13 killed and 33 wounded, with 36 horses wounded and 32 killed.

There were captured by the Mounted Troops nearly 2,000 prisoners, 14 guns and huge quantities of booty of all descriptions.

During the night the Brigade was continually sniped at from a ridge north of Beersheba. 25 prisoners, chiefly snipers, were taken by the 9th and 10th Light Horse Regiments during the night.

1st Nov. 1917

At 0500 enemy carried out an aeroplane raid; two planes flew a heavy rifle and machine gun fire from the Mounted Troops and one plane was shot down by the 8th Regiment.

Wounded and unwounded Turkish Prisoners were being taken from daylight and information gained from these that the Turks had fallen back to Sheria.

At 1430 troops of the 53rd dvision and Imperial Camel Corps moved through the outpost lines. Day outpost was then withdrawn and Brigade was concentrated in the neighbourhood of 960.

Big supplies of grain and tibbin were discovered in the vicinity of Tel el Saba. Horses were watered from pools in the Wadi Saba during the day.

At 1600 CaptainB.B. Ragless, 9th Light Horse Regiment assumed the duties of first Military Governor of Beersheba.

At 1630 "C" squadron, 9th Light Horse Regiment, moved out as escort to 1300 prisoners despatched from Beersheba to 20th Corps Headquarters at Taweil el Habari.

Convoy carrying one day's rations for man and horse arrived at Brigade Headquarters at 1800. The Brigade had left Khalasa self supporting, with supplies for three days in the event of continuous fighting, after the attack on Beersheba commenced. Two days supplies only had been used up. and the arrival of the convoy our allowed for the third days fighting ration to be carried as a day's reserve ration. Had the infantry attack on the south and the south west of Beersheba failed, this convoy could not have reached Brigade at the time it did. It travelled over that country held by the enemy up to the previous day.

The situation was now that Beersheba, the left flank of the Turkish line had been occupied by our troops. The survivors of that Garrison had fallen back towards the centre of their line at Sheria. The 2nd. Brigade had pushed on up the Beersheba-Hebron road towards Dhahariye. If more troops were sent on towards Khuweilfe the now left flank of the Turkish Line would be seriously threatened. To protect this flank the enemy would have to deplete his general reserve now in the neighborhood of Sheria. This would weaken his centre. That is what our High Command desired. The bulk of his general reserve was moved east to Khuweilfe, and a few days later our infantry broke through his unsupported line at Sheria.

In furtheranceof the above scheme orders were received for a Regiment to be attached to the 7th Mounted Brigade, (Yeomanry), for operations towards Ain Kohle and Khuweilfe, about 11 miles N.N.E. of Beersheba. These places were of tactical importance inasmuch as there was a good water supply there.

The 8th Light Horse Regiment, (Lieut.-Col. McLaurin), was detailed for this duty. The orders were that it was to go without the slightes possible delay and Division expected that it would return that night. The regimental water cart and most of the water bottles were empty. There was no time to fill them or to water the horses. The Regiment moved at 0.800.

No water cart was allowed to accompany the Regiment, and only 1 day's ration was carried. After proceeding about 9 miles the enemy were met with in position o a hill barring our progress. One Yeomanry Regiment was on our right and one on their left with a considerable distance between them.

The 8th L.H. Regt. was ordered to send one squadron to attack the enemy and drive him off the hill. The enemy was engaged and driven back about 1 mile, where strong opposition was met. The remaining 2 squadrons of the Regiment were then sent in and a line established linking up with the Yeomanry on the left.

Touch could not be gained with the Yeomanry on our right a wide valley intervening.

Our line was maintained throughout that day and night under heavy fire. On the morning of 3rd the Yeomanry Brigade was relieved by the 1st L.H. Bde of the Anzac division and the 8th L.H. Regiment came under the orders of the G.O.C. of that Brigade.

The enemy had strongly reinforced the forces opposed to us, during the night, and became very bold, but as our position was very strong, they did not attack in force.

Several attacks were by the Anzacs but were unsuccessful.

The 8th L.H. Regt. had suffered several casulties and the men were suffering severely from hunger and thirst, no water being obtainable near our position. At 1600 the 8th Regiment was relieved by Welsh Infantry and returned to Beersheba arriving in bivouac at 2300, after having been 39 hours without rest with less than 1 water bottle of water per man and rations for 2 meals. The horses were without water for the same period.

40 Cases of acute diarrhoea occured in the Regiment next day, caused, in the opinion of the Medical Officer through the drinking of large quantities of inferior water by men who were suffering severely from thirst. The Regiment was compli mented for the fine resistance it had put up under such trying circumstances.

Nov. 2.

The Brigade at 1000 had moved to half a mile south of Beersheba and employed on water developement, the chief wells had been partially destroyed by the Turks and the supply threatened to run out. Fortunately the destruction was not completed and some water could be obtained therefrom. A prisoner stated that the German Engineer who was responsible for the destruction of the wells was at the time on leave to Jerusalem.

Nov. 4.

There were probably 30,000 horses in the Beersheba area and the water question became acute There was not enough water for all there.

At 1400 the Division moved back to Karm, a distance of 15 miles. The track was in a very bad state. This route had been taken by all traffic to Beersheba from Shellal and Jemmi, throughout the four days previous. The march was most trying. The rising dust was so great that it was impossible to see the ears of one's own horse. Several casualties occured during this march, through horses and vehicles getting into uncovered wells and cisterns. At 2230 on 4th November after watering horses at Karm, the Brigade bivouaced 3/4 of a mile north west of Karm Railway Station.

Nov. 5.

The role of the Australian Mounted Division in the Karm area was :—
(a). To watch the gap between wadi Hanafish, on the right, (the left of the 20th Corps), and Hiseia, on the left, (the right of the 21st Corps).
(b). Protect the rail head which was now at Karm, and
(c). To be in readiness on the fall of the enemy's position at Hareira and Sheria to take up the pursuit.

At 0630 on 5th November 3rd Light Horse Brigade relieved the 6th Mounted Brigade, taking over the left sector—550 exclusive to Hiseia inclusive—of the Divisional Line. 9th and 10th L.H. Regiments held the day outpost lines, and both Regiments came under heavy shelling during the early part of the morning from the direction of Hareira.

Our infantry attack on Sheria was now developing, and a very heavy bombardment on Gaza could be heard. At about 1300 considerable enemy movement about 5 miles N.E. direction was observed.

On the night of 5th November 9th and 10th L. H. Regiments held the night outpost line. The night was quiet throughout.

Nov. 6.

The 8th L.H. Regiment at 0930 on 6th Novr. relieved troops from the 9th and 10th L.H. Regts. in the day outpost lines. Relief of troops continued throughout the day and all horses of the Brigade were enabled to be watered once that day at Hiseia or at Fara in the wadi Ghuzzee.

The situation along the Divisional front remained quiet but at 1100 our Infantry could be seen advancing on the Rushdi system.

At 1500 orders were received for 9th L.H. Regiment to move rapidly and take up a line on the left on the Infantry who were now well established in the Rushdie system. The line held was from Kh Kauwukah to point 510.

Enemy shelled throughout the day but only 2 casualties were inflicted on our troops. Special reconnaissances to El Magam, Khirbet um Rijl and Wadi el Baha, were made by troops from 8th L.H. Regt. during the morning, and were found clear of enemy, but enemy were observed at Atawineh. It was now evident that the enemy had fallen back everywhere on to his stronghold at Sheria.

At 1600 orders were received for 3rd A.L.H. Brigade to come under the direct of G.H.Q., and at 2300 G.H.Q. ordered the Brigade to concentrate in the vicinity of Karm in readiness for rapid movement to Sheria, via Imlieh and Irgeig

Nov. 7.

At 0730 on 7th November the Brigade, less 9th L.H. Regiment watered at Karm, and at 0815 moved at a trot and walk towards Sheria. The route taken was through Kh Imlieh and Abu Irgeig positions won from the enemy on the previous day. 9th L.H. Regiment moved from Karm at 0900, and joined up with the Brigade at point 2 miles east of Tel El Sheria station, at 1200, having covered the 16 miles from Karm in 3 hours. The Brigade now reverted to the command of the Australian Mounted Division and became Divisional reserve at a point 3/4 of a mile S.E. of Sheria station.

The enemy position at Sheria had been taken the previous day by our infantry, and evidence of severe fighting could be seen everywhere. Heavy casualties had been inflicted on the enemy here by our artillery, but our infantry casualties had also been very heavy. Sheria was still being heavily shelled by the enemy. The news that Gaza had been evacuated by the enemy had just been received. The mounted troops were now to take up pursuit of the retreating enemy.

REFERENCE MAP 1/63360, PALESTINE, SHEET XX.

At 1600 orders were received for the Brigade to move via a crossing at Kh Um El Bahr over wadi Sheria to co-operate with Anzac Division on the right and clear the ridge from that place to Kh Barrata, and wadi Saleh, which were reported held by enemy rear guards. 9th and 10th L.H. Regiments galloped on to these positions, but met with very slight enemy opposition,, it was now quite dark, the enemy had fallen back very rapidly.

Brigade outpost line with 10th L.H. Regt. on right and 9th L.H. Regiment on the left was taken up. at 2100 orders were received from Australian Mounted Division that the line wadi Jemmameh-Zuheilka, must be occupied by dawn on the 8th instant at all costs 3rd A.L.H. Bde. to connect with the left of Anzac Divn. and the right of 5th Mounted Bde. 10th L. H. Regt. gained touch with the 2nd A. L. H. Regt. but the 9th L. H. Regt. was unable to link up with the 5th Mounted Brigade as they had not occuped the position ordered. The weather continued to keep fine.

On the following morning an attempt was to be made by the mounted troops to cut off part of the main body of the retreating enemy force. The enemy had been driven from his strong defensive position Beersheba-Gaza, and his force was becoming disorganised.

Nov. 8.

At 0400 10th L.H. Regt. on the right and 9th L.H. Regt. on the left moved from night outpost line to occupy position ordered by Divisional Headquarters.

At 0450 a small enemy outpost was captured by the 9th L.H. Regt. and by 0500 just as dawn was breaking the 9th L.H. Regt. came under very heavy enemy rifle and machine gun fire. The enemy at the same time opened up a battery of 4 field guns, and the remainder of the Brigade, which had moved forward immediately in rear of the two advanced regiments were subjected to very heavy shelling. Notts battery moved back to the right flank very rapidly, and brought their guns into action immediately with good effect. 8th L.H. Regt. and remainder of M.G. Squadron and B.H.Q. group extended and moved back to a slightly covered position sustaining very few casualties. The 10th and 9th L.H. Regiments had dismounted for action on the opening up of enemy fire at 0510, and with the support of the Notts battery were pushing the Turks back, although the 9th Regiment met with strong opposition and were suffering many casulties.

The 9th L.H. Regiment, under Lieut.-Col. W. H. Scott, D.S.O., and the 10th L. H. Regiment, under Lieut.-Col. T. J. Todd, D.S.O., made a determined advance against the strong enemy position and shortly afterwards the enemy were observed to be withdrawing from his redoubt. This redoubt was now occupied by us. The Notts battery came up and gave enfilade fire against the enemy in front of the Anzac Division. During the last mentioned fighting instructions had been received from Division to move on Huj. These were now acted on, the right of the 3rd L.H. Brigade moving by Kofkah. At 0900 with the 9th L.H. Regiment in advance the Brigade moved on a bearing of 305 degrees towards Huj. At 1000 touch was gained with the 5th Mounted Brigade on our left. At 1030 the enemy were observed retiring from Huj in large numbers, but the ridges between our advanced guard and that place were held by strong rear guards. The 5th Mounted Brigade on our left now began to push vigorously towards the west of Huj. Our advanced guard conformed and with the aid of Notts Battery pushed in the opposing rear guard. The 5th Mounted Brigade were now observed to make a most gallant charge at a strong enemy position containing 4 guns and many machine guns. The charge was successful, although with heavy casualties to the Yeomanry. The right flank patrol of the 9th Regiment in charge of Lance Corporal K. C. Bennett, passed through Neby Huj at which place, after shooting one of the gun teams and capturing the remainder, two 5.9. inch modern Krupp guns were captured by that patrol.

By 1200 the whole of Huj was in our hands with much war material, together with large dumps of field and big gun ammunition. Before retiring the enemy blew up one ammunition dump, mostly S.A.A., but the vigorous action of "A" squadron of the 9th Regiment under Major Parsons, with 4 machine guns attached, prevented them from destroying others.

The whole of the enemy forces were now in full retreat. Our infantry were on our left, pursuing the Gaza garrison. The Anzac Mounted Division was on our right. The enemy on our front were making towards Simsim, and Burier, in somewhat disorganised bodies. All available squadrons of the Brigade were ordered forward, with instructions to harass the enemy, and to make what captures they could. The Notts Battery was not however, able to move past Huj, as their horses were completely exhausted, their last drink had been at Karm early the previous morning.

The three Regiments and the M.G.S. accordingly pushed forward and attacked the rear guards, inflicting heavy casualties at short range, and seizing many prisoners and guns.

From my subsequent experience of the use of the sword I consider it would have been invaluable here . If we had had swords I am sure we could have ridden on and captured thousands, as it was, we stood off and shot hundreds only. At dusk the pursuit stopped. The horses were very exhausted, they had been without water since we had left Karm 33 hours previously. It was necessary to look after them, otherwise, they would knock up, and the Brigade become immobile.

During the day 15 guns were captured by the Brigade, the following are some of the incidents of their capture:—

In square S26A. Lieut. A. Mueller, 9th L.H. Regt. with patrol, shot down the team of a 4 inch gun, and forced the escort to retire, leaving a second 4 inch gun to the right. A team of 8 bullocks was also abandoned. As these were yoked they were hitched on to the first gun but all efforts to shift it failed. The Turkish bullocks refused to assist. The gun was left and collected later on.

About the same time as the last episode, Lieut. Lilly, of the machine gun squadron, pushed his sub-section, which was attached to the 9th Light Horse Regiment well forward to the Wadi in square 072—S—17A, and shot down the team and escort of a long 10 C.M. gun, which was accordingly abandoned by the enemy.

Turks with guns were seen retreating N. W. from Jammameh. Lieut. R. H. Borbidge of the 8th L. H. Regiment galloped his troop into action, dismounting at close quarters and opening fire at the enemy with rifles and his Hotchkiss gun. The horses harnessed to one gun were shot and in the confusion the second gun fell into the Wadi. Both guns, (77 mm), together with the limbers full of ammunition and 16 prisoners were captured.

Our position was being shelled by large guns which could be seen on the Burier track, and in the Wadi where the track crosses. Fire was brought to bear on and around where the guns were firing from, at about 1500 to 1700 yards range. About 1500 in the afternoon the enemy brought up bullock teams from the Wadi with the intention of moving his gun. Lieut. McGregor, 10th L. H. Regiment went back to try and get touch with the machine gun squadron and finding Lieut. Lilly with his section with the 9th L. G. Regiment asked him to bring a Vickers gun forward to play on the enemy's teams, which he did with great effect, thus preventing guns from being moved. Lieut. McGregor then went out with his troop to try and capture the guns, but encountered such heavy machine gun and shrapnel fire on the flat that he thought it advisable to put his troop under cover whilst he went forward with a section to reconnoitre the gun position. This he did and found the gun crews and escort had broken and were retreating up the Wadi towards Simsin. He then sent back for his troop and with the remaining three men galloped up the Wadi and captured a German Officer and crew of the 6 inch Howitzer two hundred yards from the gun. Under very heavy fire he marked the gun "10th L. H. Regiment" and killed the animals, which had not already been killed by fire from our positions.

The left eight wounded Turks near the gun and brought the others in, ten in all after dark. They held the position of the day all night, and at dawn Lieut. McGregor, went out with a section of men and an A.A.M.C. detail, who dressed the wounded Turks whilst they, rounded up three Turks who were making towards Burier. Lieut. McGregor then took stock of all the gear and transport, and a description of the guns, six in all, which the different Units of the Brigade had prevented the enemy getting away. For his action in this matter Lieut. McGregor was awarded the M.C., and No. 3427, Trooper I. W. Newton was awarded the M.M.

2/Lieut. A.W.M. Thompson, 10th L. H. Regiment received orders from Major Timperley, O.C., "C" Squadron, 10th L. H. Regiment to move forward with "A" Troop, C, Squadron on the right flank together with 2/Lieut. Kingdon, on his left with "B" Troop. At this time great masses of the enemy were retreating across the flat towards Burier, in disorder. Lieut. Thompson moved his troop forward at the trot over very broken ground, skirting round a hill to the right, Lieut. Kingdon moving to the left, coming abreast of the Wadi el Hesy in square S—17.d., he was unable to get a crossing over the Wadi, so moved off to the right, and rode down the flat parallel with the wadi, those men who did not have revolvers drawing their bayonets. They charged down to what appeared to be a pretty substantial enemy transport column, about 600 yards away, the drivers and escort of which started to make off, some cutting horses out of the wagon and getting away on them. By this time shrapnel and machine gun fire were brought to bear on Lieut. Thompson's party; they then recrossed the wadi, and secured good cover for their horses. 5 prisoners were sent back to B.H.Q., with 2 of our wounded men. During this time about half a squadron of Turkish cavalry had come out and were making an attempt to get at the ammunition column. All available rifles and the Hotchkiss rifles got into action against this party, who broke and retired. The Hotchkiss rifles doing particularly good work under Sergeant Middleditch and Trooper Barrett. One troop of the 8th L. H. Regiment came into action here and took up a position on the right flank. Lieut. Thompson then decided to attempt to bring the ammunition column in. Sergeant Gwynne, Lance Corporal Hyde and Trooper Jarrick assisting. Sergeant Middleditch with the Hotchkiss Rifle and the remainder of the troop maintained a covering fire for their protection. There were 21 limbered wagons loaded with big ammunition. Some of the horses had already been shot, and some of them removed. Lieut. Thompson found it impossible to move the wagons without assistance, so to prevent the enemy removing them he shot over 60 horses. The wagons contained all large calibre ammunition. For his action in this matter Lieut. Thompson was awarded the M.C.

Lieut. L. M. S. Hargrave, 9th L. H. Regiment was in charge of B troop, A squadron, 9th L. H. Regiment. He pushed forward and occupied high ground west of junction of wadis in square 072,S,9c, and shot down part of a gun team and escort of a 15 c.m. gun. By keeping up a heavy rifle and Hotchkiss gun firehe prevented a strong enemy party reaching the guns. He later, with part of his troop, together with Lieut. P. T. Smith's troop—C troop, A squadron, 9th L. H. Regiment—charged mounted and took the gun. This would not have been possible had not Lieut. Hargrave seized the excellent tactical position he did, and broken up the enemy by fire. For his action in this matter, Lieut. Hargrave was awarded the M.C.

The Brigade suffered exceptionally light casualties in both men and horses throughout the day considering the nature of the fighting and the large number of guns, prisoners and booty won. The country was excellent for mounted operations —open, undulating, broken in parts, but not to such an extent as to block passage of mounted troops. It afforded excellent cover for mounted approach.

At about 1730 28 of our aeroplanes flew overhead in bombing formation. The noise of the explosion of the bombs dropped on the retreating enemy could be distinctly heard. The Brigade occupied the ridge two miles N.E. of Huj as a night outpost line. During the night of 8/9th November the horses of the Brigade were sent to Wadi Jemmemeh to water; this place had been made good by the Anzac Mounted Division the previous day. The supply would allow for a very slow watering, so horses were not returned to Huj until 1600 on 9th November, some of them having been thus more than 45 hours without water.

Nov. 9.

At 1630 on 9th November the following order was received from the Australian Mounted Division:—"Anzac Mounted Division is marching from Burier to Beit Duras"—"Australian Mounted Division will march from Huj station as starting point on to the line Arrak El Menshiyeh-Falujeh."

In accordance with these orders the 3rd L. H. Brigade moved at 1645 from Huj and carried out duties as advanced guard to the Division on the night march. Signallers were dropped at every half mile to guide troops in rear by flashing O.K. intermittently on the signal lamps. The route to be taken was via Northern side Kh El Hummum—Kh Zei Dan—Tel El Hesy, through very rough country. The night was dark. One of the Divisional Staff Officers doubted the ability of the Division to reach it's dawn objective by night march through country so rough that had to be crossed during the night. We had, however, often before marched by night in the presence of the enemy over unknown country by compass bearing so the Brigadier was con/dent that the Brigade, as advanced guard would be in the required position by the time ordered. At 2400 on 9th November the Brigade halted at a point on the Tur ish railway $1\frac{1}{2}$ miles south of Ara El Menshiyeh, having watered in the pools of the wadi Hesy on the way. Patrols were pushed forward and at 0100 reported Arak El Menshiyeh unoccupied by the enemy.

Nov. 10.

At 0600, 10th November, the Brigade moved forward to Arak El Menshiyeh and at 0730 the enemy opened up a battery of 6 guns on the Brigade from the direction of Zeita. A few casualties were suffered as a result of enemy shelling. It was laughable to see the rapid movements of the inhabitants of the village in taking cover when the Turkish shells burst near the village, men, women and children stampeded from the huts with shrieks and howls and promptly hid in the numerous cisterns which had been dug for storage of grain in the vicinity. The result of the air raid by our planes the previous afternoon at Arak El Menshiyeh were observed. Heaps of enemy dead and 7 burnt aeroplanes were discovered. The enemy aerodrome had been successfully bombed.

A line of observation posts were established north and north-east of Arak El Menshiyeh. Horses were taken in small numbers to water from the wells in the village. The supply was very limited and the Brigade had not completed watering by 1700. The wells were very deep, varying from 100 to 300 feet in depth. The oil engines and pumps had all been removed or totally destroyed by the enemy, and the only means of getting the water up was by buckets and ropes, a very tedious process. The enemy continued to shell the line and places of watering.

The 3rd A. L. H. Brigade was in visual communication throughout the day with the 4th A.L.H. Brigade in the neighborhood of Falujeh.

At 1200 enemy infantry, accompanied by guns was observed at Sumeil, and orders were received from the Division that the 4th A.L.H. Brigade was moving to attack the enemy, and as soon as the attack developed, the 3rd A.L.H. Brigade to pivot on right and to assist attack of the 4th A.L.H. Brigade.

At 1545 the 4th A.L.H. Brigade moved to attack Summeil from the west. The 5th Mounted Brigade from the south-west and the 3rd A.L.H. Brigade from the south. By dark, (1715), the attack had not fully developed, delay took place in getting in touch with the 4th A.L.H. Brigade, and it was decided that the Brigades would not push in the dark.

Supply columns were now finding it difficult to keep up with the mounted troops in their rapid advance. Rations began to be received by the forward troops late, and immediately on being off loaded had to be taken up to the troops in the front line, sometimes under heavy fire. Through the later, and later arrival of the rations, one day's rations were lost to men and horses, as in the army arrears of rations are never made up.

At 2000 the Brigade held the following battle night out post line:—
Arak El Menshiyeh to railway bridge V7d sheet 1/63360, (8th L.H. sector,

9th L.H. sector). Enemy fired many flares from the direction of Summeil throughout the night.

Nov. 11.

At 0430 the Brigade stood to arms. The situation was quiet. The 10th A.L.H. Regiment tok over the outpost line from 9th and 8th L.H. Regiments who on relief proceeded to water at Arak El Menshiyeh, and draw rations.

At 0500 patrols from 9th L.H. Regiment and Brigade scouts were pushed forward from the outpost line to reconnoitre Summeil, and at 0600 occupied that place and found it clear of the enemy.

At 0730 patrols were in communication with Yeomanry Division on the right and 4th A.L.H. Brigade on the left. The situation along the entire front remained quiet, and no enemy activity was observed.

At 0930 enemy was observed in strength holding high ridge $1\frac{1}{2}$ miles north-east of Summeil, and commenced shelling Summeil from a position on high ground about 3 miles east. Patrols reconnoitred further forward, and came under heavy rifle and machine gun fire from these positions, and also from the high ridge 1 mile further north. It was now seen that the enemy had re-organised and was determined to make a stand with this rear guard. 10th A.L.H. Regiment was ordered to carry out active patrolling, making itself as conspicuous as possible, without becoming seriously engaged, the object to attract attention to a line then held while the remainder of the Division moved north.

At 1700 10th A.L.H. Regiment occupied night outpost line Arrak El Menshiyeh to Summeil, linking up with the 5th Mounted Brigade on the right and 4th A.L.H. Brigade on the left, and were relieved by 8th L.H. Regiment by 2400.

Nov. 12.

At stand to arms at 0430 the situation along the Divisional front was still quiet and at 0600 one squadron 9th L.H. Regiment under Major Parsons moved from Felujeh to reconnoitre Berkusie from the S.W. 8th L.H. Regiment maintained a line of observation posts and watched for any enemy movements on the roads leading from Arrak El Manshiyeh—Beit Jibrin road. Dust had been observed rising from direction of Jibrin since daylight.

At 0830 the reconnoitring squadron of 9th L.H. Regiment occupied Berkusie without encountering enemy opposition. Information was here gained from the inhabitants that enemy estimated at 5,000 in strength, with machine and field guns had withdrawn to Tel El Safi at 2200 on the previous night.

Watering of as many horses of the Brigade as possible was now aimed at. The supply at Ijseir and Hatte was very limited, and at 1330 when orders were received from Division for the Brigade to be prepared for immediate action, very few horses or men had been given a drink.

About 6,000 enemy infantry were now reported to be advancing from Et Tine. Troop trains were observed unloading infantry and enemy cavalry were moving to the west of Balin. Orders were received from Division for one Regiment to move to a point one mile S.W. of Summeil, and support 5th Mounted Brigade which was to meet the enemy advance at Balin. The enemy appeared in strength all along the front and threatened a determined attack. The Notts battery co-operated with all batteries of the Division in maintaining fire against the enemy, whose advance was being covered by his own artillery from many batteries.

The role of our Division was to hold firmly the right flank of the general advance so that the centre and left could push forward without anxiety for their right flank. From enemy documents since captured the advance of the Turks just mentioned was an organised attack on our right flank. They hoped that it would be successful. If it had, it would have seriously affected the advance of the rest of our forces now moving northwards on our left and along the coast.

At about 1400 the enemy attack had developed.

5th Mounted Brigade was being heavily pressed by the enemy. 9th Light Horse Regiment was now holding Berkusie ridge, and although attacked time after time, continued to check the determined advance of the Turks. One squadron, 8th Light Horse Regiment was sent to the assistance of the 5th Mounted Brigade and the remaining two squadrons to the assistance of the 9th Regiment, where, was now heavily engaged and suffering many casualties.

At 1600, 10th Light Horse Regiment, who had been sent to Falujey to water horses was now brought up at the gallop on account of the general situation, and 'C' Squadron thereof was put on the right of the 9th Light Horse Regiment. Owing to enemy pressure on the left the 5th Mounted Brigade was forced to retire, and the 8th and 9th Light Horse Regiments, with 10th Light Horse Regiment supporting on the right, were now compelled to conform and to fall back on to the next ridge, i.e.—the one between Summeil and Berkusie Ridges. As soon as the ridge from which the enemy advance had been checked by 8th and 9th Regiments was retired from, the enemy with extreme boldness occupied same. It was discovered that some wounded had been left behind when the retirement from Berkusie ridge was made and Sergeant James Bowman of the 1th Light Horse Regiment and Lieut. T. M. Rickaby, 3rd Brigade Scout Officer, returned and rescued wounded, the former being subsequently granted the D.C.M. for his action in this affair.

At 1700 the Turkish attack died away. The night outpost line, (9th L.H. Regiment on the left, and 8th L.H. Regiment on the right), from Arrak El Menshiyeh to Summeil was taken up. The Brigade had taken part in a day's very heavy fighting and all ranks and horses were in much need of rest and sleep, little of which had been gained for the past several days, and nights. The question of water for horses was again becoming very acute. The night, 12/13th November passed quietly and at stand to arms at 0430 there was no enemy activity.

Nov. 13.

At 0645, 13th November, enemy were observed to be holding Berkusie ridge in strength, and small enemy parties were dribbling forward on to the low hills north-east of Summeil. The Brigade held the line Arrak El Menshiyeh—Summeil with 8th Light Horse Regiment on right sector and 9th Light Horse Regiment on left sector, and 10th Light Horse Regiment concentrated in neighborhood of B.H.Q. Four sub-sections of the Machine Gun Squadron were placed in support of the troops in the line, and the remainder in the vicinity of B.H.Q. Notts battery opened fire on to Berkusie ridge, shelling the enemy with good effect. The continuation of the strong attack of the previous day was expected, and the Brigade was in readiness. At 1300 the enemy were observed to be once again in retreat. The 3rd A.L.H. Brigade were ordered to extend the line north-east to Sherklye and watch for enemy movements from the direction of Beit Jibrin and Zeita. The line held now by the Brigade was the right flank of the mounted force in pursuit. 4th A.L.H. Brigade and 7th Mounted Brigade took up the attack on the enemy on the left, but owing to the exhausted condition of the men and horses the attack was abandoned.

At 1730 night outpost lines from point 248 to Sherklye was taken up, and at 1800 B.H.Q. was established 1 mile south of Tel El Turmus. ,The line was lightly held, rest for as many troops as possible being aimed at. The night 13/14th November was quiet throughout.

Nov. 14

The brigade stoodto arms at 0430 and at 0645, 14th November, 10th L.H. Regt. established a line of observation posts from Tel el Turmus to point 248, the remainder of the Brigade concentrated and at 0830 marched to Wadi Sucerier, north of Esdud, a distance of 10 miles where there was a plentiful supply of water.

At 1300 the Brigade, less 10th L.H. Regiment arrived at Wadi Sucerier. The Brigade Engeneers had preceded the main body, and had erected troughs in readiness for the watering of the Brigade in the fine lagoons which exist near the mouth of this Wadi. The Brigade bivouaced 1 mile east of Neby Younis, and received orders to keep in readinesse to march at short notice for operations nortwards. All ranks at once set about bathing and washing clothes; this was the first time since moving out for operations on 28th October that water had been found to permit of washing. On account of continued action with the enemy, rations had not been able to be kept up to all forward troops regularly. There was opportunity now for cooking, sheep were purchased by our troops from the local inhabitants and the fresh meat was appreciated. Bread, (brown), was also obtainable, and augmented the short issue of biscuits which had been unavoidable on account of continued active operations.

Nov. 15.

The Brigade enjoyed a much needed rest. At 1445 10th L.H. Regiment rejoined the Brigade from night outpost duty point 248—Te El Tumus line. 10th A.L.H. Regiment horses had been kept saddled for 2 whole days and nights and had been without water for that period. On examination of the horses of the Brigade, only a very small percentage of sore backs was disclosed. There had been very few opportunities for off saddling of horses ever since the morning of the 7th November when the Brigade moved from Karm area.

Nov. 16.

The Brigade continued to rest, but was kept in readiness to move at short notice Horses were watered as often as they would drink. The weather kept fine, and the rain still held off. Men and horses were feeling the benefit of the resting, the full rations were now being received. Attention was given to mending and adjusting of saddlery and equipment.

Nov. 17.

At 1000 the Brigade moved en route for Wadi Surbar, preparatory to relieving 7th Mounted Brigade at El Kubab early the following morning, (18th November). The Brigade halted at 1530, and bivouaced in the vicinity of Junction Station and received orders to be prepared to move at half an hours notice from 0600 on 18th November. The enemy was found to be holding Latron and Amwas in strength, and an attack on these places was to be carried out on the morning of 18th November by the Australian Mounted Division. The low hills and undulating country were now left. Latron and Amwas were the first places in the more mountainous parts to which the enemy had fallen back.

Nov. 18.

At 0500 9th Light Horse Regiment with two sub-sections machine guns moved forward to relieve Regiment of 7th Mounted Brigade at El Kubab. The Yeomanry Mounted Division would operate against the enemy to the north whilst the Australian Mounted Division was directed on Latron and Amwas.

At 0800 the remainder of the Brigade moved forward and reached Kubab at 1100, coming under enemy shelling. Patrols from 9th Light Horse Regiment were sent east and north-east, and gained touch with the left of the Yeomanry Division at Annabeh. Owing to the mountainous nature of the country, great difficulty was being experienced in moving to the required position. The guns and wheeled ambulance had to be left to the north of Amwas. Horses had to be led as the ground was too rocky to ride them. 4th Light Horse Brigade was to co-operate on the right of the 3rd Light Horse Brigade. One squadron 9th Light Horse Regiment was directed on Bir Main—Beit Sira to maintain communication with the 8th Mounted Brigade on their left. The remainder of the 9th Regiment moved to occupy Yalo, and Beir Eyub with a view to cut the main Latron—Jerusalem road beyond Latron. The 8th Light Horse Regiment in moving to support the 9th Light Horse Regiment also came under artillery fire. Owing to the rough and rocky nature of the locality, the movement of the Mounted Troops became very difficult and touch with flanking troops was continually lost. The 9th Light Horse Regiment was unable to reach it's objective in the rear of the Turkish position owing to the heavy fire from numerous machine guns which the Turks had emplaced on the right flank of their position. Sergeant Masson of the 9th Regiment with a patrol reconnoitred Yalo village and reported that place clear but high ground to east strongly held by enemy.

At 1625 the Divisional Commander ordered a general withdrawal. The guns of the Notts battery had been pushed as far forward as the ground would allow. This proved a difficult task and the guns had taken considerable hauling over the rough country. The gunners were well rewarded with good targets and the guns were kept in action throughout the afternoon at a range of 5,000 yards. Enemy guns in Latron were silenced at 1530. Enemy then attempted to manhandle his guns and withdraw them, but rapid fire was opened up, and the enemy was dispursed, without removing the guns. The Notts battery had fired 189 rounds during the afternoon. On the advance of the infantry the following day they found 4 enemy guns were abandoned.

At 1800 the Brigade had withdrawn and commenced to march back to the previous night's bivouac in the vicinity of Junction Station, a distance of 13 miles. Movement through and from the high and rocky hills was very slow. 2 water carts and 3 sand carts, (two carrying wounded), collapsed, and many horses were lamed. At 2230 the Brigade bivouaced.

Nov. 19.

The Brigade rested throughout the day, horses being watered once only. Soon after 0600 the sky became overcast, and heavy clouds portended the downfall which was now so long overdue. By 1500 a heavy rain had set and continued throughout the night, 19/20th November. The camping places soon became quagmires, and the wintry conditions were felt by all ranks and the horses. Transport difficulties were now to be faced on account of the boggy condition of the ground?

The Brigadier was informed that the 3rd Light Horse Brigade would probably represent Australia in the forces to be detailed for the capture of Jerusalem.

Nov. 21.

Instructions were received from the Australian Mounted Division for 1 Regiment of the 3rd A.L.H. Brigade to join the 5th Mounted Brigade for operations against Jerusalem, and the 10th Light Horse Regiment being at the time the strongest Regiment in the Brigade in personnel and horses were despatched.

The Gloucester Yeomanry, 5th Mounted Brigade, became attached to the 3rd A L.H. Brigade in lieu of the 10th.

The following is a precise of the operations carried out by the 10th Light Horse Regiment, from the time of the detachment from 3rd A.L.H. Brigade on the morning of the 21st November, 1917, to the time of rejoining the Brigade on the 14th December, 1917.

Reference map 1/63360, Palestine map sheet XVII.

At 1400 21st November 10th Light Horse Regiment, (Lieut.-Col. T. J. Todd, D.S.O.), joined up with 5th Mounted Brigade at Latron and watered and fed up soon after. At 1600 the march to Bab El Wad along the Jerusalem road was commenced. It was now raining very heavily and continued throughout the night 5th Mounted Brigade bivouaced at Bab El Wad just clear of the pass. A fearful congestion of traffic all along the road existed. Transport with supplies was in difficulties everywhere, on account of the condition of the road brought about by heavy traffic, rain and enemy shelling.

Nov. 22.

At 0600 the march forward was continued but in order to pass the transport waggons along the only road, the Regiment had to advance in single file, and it was 1500 before Saris was reached. The 5th Mounted Brigade bivouaced at Saris for the night Horses were watered from the native wells under constant enemy shelling, but no casualties were suffered. It rained heavily throughout the day and the temperature was very cold.

Nov. 23.

At 0600 1 squadron 10th Light Horse Regiment under Major Dunckley moved through the 75th Division to Enab and Soba, from where patrols were sent eastward to Ain Karim, and Jura, and southwards to Setaf. The country was stoney and precipitous and great difficulty was experienced in moving horses which invariably had to be led.

At 1500 patrols returned to bivouac at Saris bringing 13 Turkish prisoners captured while on outpost at Ain Karim. Much useful information had been gained of the enemy throughout the day both by reconnaissance and from the inhabitants. A second squadron 10th L.H. Regiment was despatched at 0700 to occupy Bidu, and was heavily shelled in carrying out the task. Relay posts were established between Bidu and headquarters at Enab and these too were heavily shelled. The squadron remained at Bidu until the following morning, (24th Nov.), and was then relieved by C squadron and returned to Enab. The remaining two squadrons, 10th L. H. Regiment, moved to Soba at 0700 on 24th November to carry out strong reconnaissance towards Bittir railway station, it was reached at 1200. Enemy commenced shelling but no casualties were suffered. It was discovered that the station buildings at Bittir had recently been demolished and the centre span of railway bridge west of station blown away. Information was gained from Bedouins that 200 Turks had been at these places the previous day and carried out demolition work, afterwards retiring. Information gained by the reconnaissance proved that the enemy were not holding any position in force west of Bittir. The camp at Saris was reached at 1800. Both men and horses were very tired. Temperature was still very low but rain held off.

Nov. 25.

C squadron returned from Bidu and moved to Ammur where they were outposted on high ground at K.H. Loz.

Nov. 26.

It was found impossible to keep up rations to a whole Brigade of Mounted Troops in the hills, and all except 10th Light Horse Regiment returned to the plains. The 60th Division had now taken over from the 75th Division. The 75th Division had suffered very heavy casualties in their operations in this area. The enemy had to be attacked in his positions on the high points. At 1200 on 27th November the Regiment reached Artuf where a plentiful supply of water was found. The place was a Jewish settlement and centre of considerable importance. Delicious pastry was here purchased by the troops from the inhabitants, who welcomed the British troops.

On 28th November a reconnaissance southwards to red Roman road and along the Wadi Najal was carried out.

On 29th November the Regiment was employed making a track for wheeled traffic along Wadi Najal reconnoitred the previous day.

On 29th and 30th November the country along the Jerusalem railway, embracing Welejeh—Bittir—Kuryet—Saidee—Aquarl—Khudr—Housan—El Kabu—Kh. Yehudi—Kh Tazah—Erras was reconnoitred. Enemy was being encountered but not in strength, and shots were continually exchanged. Efforts to drive the Turks from Bittir and Welejeh were unsuccessful on account of enemy commanding the high ground north of these places.

On 1st December the 10th Light Horse Regiment continued reconnoitring, most of which had to be done on foot, it was impossible to get horses over the country. Reconnaissance to Erras disclosed abundant supply of water at that place, and at 0600 1 squadron, 10th Light Horse Regiment moved from Artuf to establish itself at Erras, and carry out reconnaissance to Bittir—Welejeh—Khudr—Hausan and towards Beit Jala and the Hebron road. Natives were very friendly towards our troops, and much information of the enemy was gained.

On 2nd December 10th Light Horse Regiment was inspected by Major-General Shea, D.S.O., commanding 60th Division. On 2/3rd December active patrolling was carried out. Enemy continually being encountered and prisoners broughtin as result.

On 4th December Lieut.-Col. Todd, D.S.O., 10th L. H. Regiment proceeded to Enab from Artuf to attend meeting of Unit Commanders at 60th Divisional headquarters to discuss projected operations against Jerusalem. The role allotted to the 10th Light Horse Regiment was principally to link up with 53rd Infantry Division which was to advance up the Hebron road past Bethlehem and attack Jerusalem from the south and from the south-east.

On 4th, 5th, 6th and 7th December active patrolling was continued.

On 8th December the final assault on Jerusalem by 53rd Division on the right and 60th Division on the left with 10th Light Horse Regiment linking up both Divisions was launched; all ranks of 10th Light Horse Regiment had been engaged on continuous duties for many days and nights, during which time rain and wind squalls prevailed. The thoughts of entering Jerusalem counteracted all personal discomforts. Later on, the night of 8th December, troops of the 53rd Division, succeeded in entering the city after strenuous fighting. The weather remained wet and squally.

On 9th December the 10th L. H. Regiment entered Jerusalem, and established themselves as the first mounted British troops in the Holy City.

On 10th and 11th December the 10th Light Horse Regiment carried out strong reconnaissance towards Awata—Hazmeh—Jeba and Ran, drawing heavy enemy fire on each occasion when these places were approached. Although Jerusalem had been captured from the Turks, the enemy had not fallen back to any considerable extent, and a counter attack was prepared for.

At 1200 on 11th December the formal entry by British troops into Jerusalem, headed by the Commander-in-Chief, General Sir Edmund Allenby, G.C.B., was made. Military and political representatives of France and Italy and all British Dominions with troops on the Palestine front accompanied the C.-in-C. Captain H. V. Throssel, V.C., and 30 other ranks of the 10th Light Horse Regiment represented Australia in the allied armies, which formed up at the Jaffa gate for the entrance of the procession into the Holy City.

At 0730 on 13th December the 10th L. H. Regiment became detached from 20th Army Corps, and marched out of Jerusalem en route to join 3rd Light Horse Brigade which had been operating dismounted in the hilly country in the neighborhood of El Burj since 29th November. In passing General Headquarters the Commander-in-Chief took the salute of the Regiment and thanked the Commanding Officer on behalf of the Regiment for its valuable work in co-operation with the infantry leading up to the fall and occupation of Jerusalem, and congratulated Lieut.-Col. Todd, D.S.O., on having the honour of commanding the first British Cavalry Regiment to enter Jerusalem.

At 1615 on 13th December Latron was reached where horses were watered and rations and forage drawn, and the Regiment bivouaced for the night. At 0830 the Regiment moved from Latron and re-joined 3rd Light Horse Brigade at 1120 at Hariyeh. The Brigade was now operating as a dismounted unit, and 10th Light Horse Regiment horses were sent back to Katra with proportion of 1 man to 4 horses.

On the detachment of 10th Light Horse Regiment and attachment of Gloucester Yeomanry Regiment, on 20th November, orders were received for the Brigade to move back to Mejdel the following morning.

Nov. 21.

Reference map—Palestine 1/63360, *sheet XVI.*

At 1000 the Brigade, less 10th Light Horse Regiment, with Gloucester Yeomanry attached moved from garden well in vicinity of Junction Station en route for Mejdel, a march of 20 miles. The Brigade reached Mejdel and bivouaced. The weather now was fine, the ground was boggy and transport difficulties were experienced.

A plentiful supply of water was available and supplies were received regularly. The re-fitting of the Brigade and clipping of horses were proceeded with.

A party of representatives from each Unit of the Brigade was sent back to the Brigade dumps at Gamli and Shellal, to procure men's blankets, bivvies, and stores, urgently required, and which could not be readily procured from Ordnance. The weather remained fine. The camping area at Mejdel was well drained, and the effects of the previous heavy rains were not experienced.

A large mail, letters, papers and parcels were received on the 26th November, the first for over a month. The contents of the parcels were very highly appreciated.

Canteen stores were unprocurable and the eatables sent from overseas formed a very much needed variation of diet. The troops had been on mobile rations bully beef, biscuit and jam for over a month.

Nov. 27.

At 1800 on 27th November, orders were received from the Division for the Brigade to march at 2230 that night, and proceed to Kh Deiran, a march of 22 miles, and remain in readiness to move into the front line at Berfilya or Shilta, where the enemy were heavily counter-attacking.

At 2215 the Brigade commenced it night's march to Deiran, and reached that place at 0700 on 28th November.

Nov. 28.

The Brigade rested in the vicinity of Deiran throughout the day. The Brigadier was informed by the Divisional Commander that the enemy had driven the 54th Division from Shilta, and the 3rd Light Horse Brigade was to be prepared to march at a moments notice to the neighborhood of Berfilya, and support the infantry.

At 2345, 28th November, orders were received from the Division for the 3rd Light Horse Brigade less 10th Regiment, and Notts Battery, but with Gloucester Yeomanry Regiment attached, to move at once, march to Berfilya and come under the orders of the G.O.C., 52nd Division on arrival.

At 0015 on 29th November the Brigade commenced it's second successive night march and reached Berfilya a distance of 13 miles at 0530.

Nov. 29.

The Brigade on arrival at Berfilya was without waiting further instructions to take up a position to cover Berfilya from the N.E., and to push out patrols to gain touch with the 52nd Division on the right and the 54th Division on the left. The 9th Light Horse Regiment acted as advanced guard to the Brigade on this march, and pushed out patrols from Berfilya and located the 155th infantry Brigade of 52nd Division at El Burj, and gained touch with the right of the 54th Division, about $1\frac{1}{2}$ miles north of Berfilya?

At 0830 the Brigadier proceeded to Headquarters, 52nd Division at Beit Nuba to attend conference of 20th Corps Commander at that place, and received orders for the future movement of the Brigade. Nose bags were put on the horses, and men took the opportunity to rest. Both men and horses were tired after two successive night marches.

At 1245 the Brigadier returned to the Brigade at Berfilya and explained the requirements of the Divisional Commander. The 3rd Light Horse Brigade dismounted, was to take over the line held by the 155th infantry Brigade and to establish it's headquarters at El Burj. The only horses to remain in the hills were to be pack horses ammunition transport, and water cart horses.

At 1530 the Brigade moved from Berfilya to El Burj, (2 miles), and at 1630 the men were dismounted, seconds in command of Regiments, 6 officers per Regiment, and 1 man to 4 horses, returned to Kh Deiran, with the horses of the Brigade.

The sight of Light horsemen marching into the line with full kit up brought back memories of old Gallipoli days. The thoughts of "footing" it everywhere and being away from their horses, were unpleasant to some of the men. However, within a fortnight the opinion of the majority had changed. Heavy rains, mud, and wintry conditions generally set in and it was agreed that under such conditions with horses to attend to, life would have been miserable indeed. From the commencement of the desert fighting, only one short period of a week of wet weather had been experienced and this was when the Brigade was operating back in the sand. The sloppy conditions were altogether new.

By 2200, 3rd Light Horse Brigade had taken over from the 155th Infantry Brigade, the line from a point 1 1/4 miles south-east of El Burj and $\frac{1}{2}$ mile north of El Burj, to Kh Abu Fureij, 1 mile north-west of El Burj. The Brigade had been considerably reduced in numbers by casualties, and an epidemic of diarrhoea since moving out on operations on 28th November, and had not yet been reinforced, consequently the above line could only be thinly held. 8th Light Horse Regiment took over the right sector and 9th Light Horse Regiment the left sector. During night 29/30th November the Brigade were sniped at and shelled intermittently from Shilta and Suffa.

Nov. 30.

At stand to arms at 0430 the situation was quiet and remained so throughout the day. Very little enemy activity was observed with the exception of an occasional burst of machine gun fire from Shilta, and intermittent shelling by 2 small field guns from Suffa.

At 1900, 4th Light Horse Brigade took over the right half of the line held by the 3rd Light Horse Brigade. The 8th Light Horse Regiment and 9th Light Horse Regiment closed on the left of the 9th Light Horse Regiment and the section of the line now held by the Brigade was strengthened.

On 155th Infantry Brigade being relieved from the line, 1/4th R.S. Fusiliers under Lieut. Col. Stewart Richardson, remained as reserve to the 3rd A.L.H. Brigade. At 2200, 29th November this battalion reverted to the command of the 52nd Division, but remained in the vicinity of B.H.Q. at El Burj.

The strength of the Brigade in personnel and horses at the time was as follows:—

	In the hills.			At Deiran with led horses.		
	Off.	O/rs.	Horses.	Off.	O/rs.	Horses.
B.H.Q.	4	19	13	1	13	35
Scouts	—	13	—	—	4	18
3rd Sig. Troop	1	20	1	—	17	39
8th L.H. Regt.	16	198	46	6	169	443
9th L H. Regt.	13	206	50	9	169	439
3rd M.G.S.	7	94	57	1	103	226
3rd L.H. F.A.	4	43	30	2	29	62
3rd Field Troop	1	8	4	1	38	58
Totals	46	601	201	20	542	1320
Gloucester Yeo (Two squads)	8	127	38	5	90	283
Grand Total..	54	728	239	25	632	1603

10th Light Horse Regiment detached with 60th Divn. Notts Battery detached with 54th Division.

The weather was remaining fine and dry. Bivouacing in the stoney hills was a new experience. Men not actually on observation post gained good rest during the day.

An enemy attck on that part of the line now held by the Australian Mounted Division was expected and preparations were made for such by getting reserve of ammunition sent into the lines. Every available rifle man was now either in the front or support line. Transport horses and vehicles of the Brigade were grouped together and remained under cover of the high hills 500 yards S.W. of El Burj. Although the enemy had shelled this area intermittently throughout the day no casualties were incurred. The majority of the enemy shells burst to the rear.

From 2000 to 2400, 30th November, the situation was very quiet, the enemy only occasionally sniped and shelled at positions, but no incident happened either during the day or evening which pointed to the determined attack, which the enemy made on our position soon after midnight.

1st Dec.

At 0100 from the post of the 8th Light Horse Regiment on the extreme right of the Brigade sector considerable movement in its immediate front was observed and reported.

At 0110 the enemy, estimated 500 in strength, attacked the above mentioned post with hand and rifle grenades. On the 8th Light Horse Regiment calling for artillery support by means of flares at 0130 the 268th Brigade, R.F.A., and the Hong Kong and Singapore mountain battery opened up intense artillery fire on all enemy approaches. Part of the Gloucester Yeomanry, 48 all ranks, intrength, under the command of Lieut.-Col. Palmer, D.S.O., moved from the position at El Burj to support the 8th Light Horse Regiment and at 0150 reinforced the 8th Light Horse Regiment in the fighting line where the fighting had now developed.

At 0200 the 8th Light Horse Regiment post on the right was forced to withdraw 200 to 300 yards toward the main line of defence. The enemy was now attacking heavily and pressed on toward the main line of defence, using bombs of both cricket ball and stick type, rifle grenades and automatic rifles. Their advance was covered by an enemy battery firing from Suffa, and one trench mortar firing from the neighborhood of Shilta. At this time Lieut.-Col. Stewart Richardson commanding 1/4th Royal Scots Fusiliers came to Brigade Headquarters and offered the assistance of his infantry, (who were not now under the command of the Brigade); this officer was gladly accepted, and two companies, 130 all ranks, were sent to the support of the 8th Light Horse Regiment. An exceptionally fine feeling of comradship had ever existed between the Scotch and Australian troops but this would be the first occasion in the campaign when they had fought together.

At 0230 one of the above companies of the 1/4th Royal Scots Fusiliers reinforced the 8th Light Horse Regiment and at once operated with Mills grenades with great effect, and assisted materially in holding up the enemy attack.

At 0300 the enemy was held up within 30 yards of our main position, throughout the attack the 9th Light Horse Regiment was bringing enfilade fire, with rifles machine guns, and Hotchkiss rifles, to bear on the enemy.

At 0315 the enemy appeared to be held. At this time the second company 1/4th Royal Scots Fusiliers reached 8th Light Horse Regimental Headquarters. The bombers were at once detached and immediately put into the firing line.

At 0400 the enemy fire and bombing had considerably decreased. The attack had failed.

At 0520 a large party of enemy were observed under cover in front of our positions. Their retirement had been prevented by the enfilade fire of the 9th Light Horse Regiment and the machine guns attached.

On movement towards this party by 8th Light Horse Regiment a machine gun and Hotchkiss rifle barrage was put down by 9th Light Horse Regiment from their position on the left front. Our two batteries put down a barrage behind the enemy also. This party surrendered and 105 unwounded prisoners were captured, among them being the Commanding Officer of the Battalion.

Our total casualties were 56, of which 39 were in the 8th Light Horse Regiment. 17 Wounded Turkish prisoners were brought in during the day.

A captured Medical Officer stated that the attacking forces consisted of the assault battalion of the 19th Division and that exclusive of the wounded which had been evacuated by him early in the fight, there were none of the Battalion left. A few days later three men, who said they belonged to this battalion, came in and surrendered, saying that their comrades were either killed or with us as prisoners, and that they were lonely and wanted to join the later.

This assault battalion consisted of specially picked troops, their physique was the best we had ever seen amongst Turkish prisoners. The battalion had only arrived a few days before from the Galician front. They were all armed with bombs and most of them wore German type of steel helmet. One man had thrown 92 bombs, (as was evidence by the number of metal clips), before he was shot through the head.

Included in the captured material were 8 automatic rifles, similar in pattern, to our own Hotchkiss rifles.

For service in this action the following decorations were awarded:—Captain MacPherson and Lieut. Peppercorn, military crosses; S.S.M. Currington and Trooper Keeble, D.C.M's.

At 0600, 1st December, the original line held by the Brigade, was re-occupied.

The situation became quiet with intermittent enemy shelling and machine gunning.

Congratulations on the good fight put up were received from the 20th Corps and Desert Mounted Corps Commanders during the day. Parties burying, own and enemy dead were kept busy throughout the day. Enemy dead in front of our position had to remain unburied for several days. On attempting to reach the bodies our troops came under very heavy enemy machine gun and rifle fire.

At 1700 on 1st December, 1/4th Royal Scots Fusiliers moved from the 3rd A.L.H. Brigade area at El Burj, and marched to Latron. Cheers were exchanged between the Scotchmen and the Australians as the former moved off. One Scott was heard by his C.O. to say to another :—"Those are the sort of men I like to support, you will find them in the firing line when you get up there to support them—you won't have to bring them back with you."

The disposition of the Brigade remained—8th Light Horse Regiment holding right sector, 9th Light Horse Regiment left sector, and Gloucester Yeomanry in support 400 yards north of El Burj. A state trench warfare now existed, but in place of trenches, stone sangars were erected. The Turks occupied Shilta—Belain and Suffa, but gradually fell back on to the line Kuddis—Kurbeth—Ibn—Harith—Kefr Namah. Until 27th December, Australian Mounted Division held the sector of the line opposite these places, gradually pushing the line forward and consolidating. Two of the 3rd, 4th and 5th Brigades were relieved in turns for a few days from the line by the third one during this period. The Headquarters of the 3rd Brigade were established at several different places in the area. Heavy rains fell and much discomfort and cold were experienced by all ranks. Life in the rocky and high hills was now the extreme of that spent for so long in the sands of the Sinai desert. Supplies were received regularly but often there was an unavoidable short issue. Supply columns between rail head and Latron often failed to get through on account of the boggy nature of the only available tracks. The enemy showed very little activity; close observation was being kept.

The enemy's positions at Kefr Namah—Harith—Jurdeh and Kuddis were daily shelled by our artillery. Any appearance of enemy in his defence works would immediately be followed by the opening of our guns on to him, and he now always aimed for concealment. Any additional work to his defences were carried out during the night. The situation all along the Divisional line became exceptionally quiet,. only an occasional machine gun burst could be heard. Sniping and rifle fire had practically ceased.

Although wet and wintry conditions prevailed, all ranks were gradually bivouacing under more comfort. Many were forced to remain wet for several days, but all were now becoming more or less used to these conditions. Strong defences, (chiefly sangars), were built all along the line. Enemy aeroplanes became active and two or three times daily flew over our lines, sometimes at a low altitude.

On 12th December advice was received that enemy aeroplanes had raided and bombed the horse camp, (1 mile east of Surafend)—at 1500 on the previous day and at 0700 that day, 12th December, inflicting casualties of 7 other ranks wounded and 34 horses killed, and 58 wounded. The Brigade horses were moved from Deiran to Ludd, and thence to Katra. Camp areas quickly became quagmires, and the horses were feeling the cold and wintry conditions very much. The issue of forage was short, very often on account of transport difficulties along the line of communication and for a period of 11 days the issue of grain was reduced to one half, and tibbin was often not an issue. With 1 man to 4 horses the attention given to horses was limited, and the Brigade horses went back considerably in condition and appearance.

Reference map—Palestine sheet 1/63360, *sheet* 17.

Dec. 14.

10th Light Horse Regiment rejoined the Brigade from on detachment with 20th Corps at Jerusalem, (see account of 10th L.H. Regiment operations previous). Only occasionally, and then very little, was enemy movement observed. Road and track making in Wadi Muslieb were proceed with.

On 21st December reconnaissance by Brigadier and Regimental Commanders was carried out and as an intermediate line of defence between enemy and our own position a line along the high ridge on south of and overlooking wadi Sad was selected. From information gained from deserters and prisoners it was leannt that the Turks were holding the line Namah—Harith—Jurdeh—Kuddis with dismounted cavalry and that many of these were being transferred to Ramallah and Birgeh. The enemy was massing his troops in these areas in preparation for a big counter attack against Jersualem. The rain and wintry conditions continued and wintry conditions continued and slight shortages of rations were being experienced.

Dec. 23.

On 23rd December information had been received by General Headquarters that the enemy intended to attack on Christmas Day with the object of regaining Jersualem, and the Brigade was ordered to stand to in readiness to co-operate with the 29th Infantry Brigade (10th Division) on the right.

On 24th December it rained unceasingly all day. A parcel and letter mail was received from the led horse camp now at Katra. This day and on the morning of Christmas Day, Christmas gifts from the A.I.F. Comforts Funds arrived, and were immediately distributed to the troops. The goods received were chiefly eatables, and at such a time were very highly appreciated by all ranks. Christmas Day, 1917, well be remembered by members of the Brigade who were on the hills at the time as one of the wettest and one of the coldest days ever experienced on active service.

Reference map—Palestine 1/63360, *sheet* 14.

Dec. 26.

At 1100 orders were received from the Division to occupy by 1745 a line half mile north of Wadi Sad, ,from the wadi Shamy on the left, in support of and in co-operation with 29th infantry Brigade on the right, carrying out operations to occupy Namah ridge. 10th Light Horse Regiment on right and 9th A.L.H. Regt. on left occuped this line at 1745 as ordered. This constituted the first in series of stages in operations to be carried out against the enemy to prevent him from transferring his troops eastward.

At 1930 an advanced line with 10th Light Horse Regiment on right sector and 9th Light Horse Regiment on left sector was occupied as night outpost line. The situation was quiet throughout the night.

Dec. 27.

At 0835 main defensive line from Belain eastward to wadi Shamy was occupied with 10th Light Horse Regiment holding right sector and 9th L.H. Regiment left sector. Touch was gained with 6th Royal Irish Fusiliers on the right and 11th Light Horse Regt. on left. Enemy shelled neighbourhood of B.H.Q. but otherwise there was only slight enemy activity in front of the Brigade sector. 29th Infantry Bde. was meeting with strong enemy opposition in their advance to occupy the Namah ridge. The demonstrating patrols pushed forward by 10th L.H. Regt. and 9th L.H. Regt from the main defensive line reached line north of wadi Shamy, drawing machine gun and rifle fire from enemy positions at Khurbetha Ibn Harith. On strong patrols of the 10th L. H. Regt. threatening the right flank of the Turgs on Namah ridge the latter withdrew.

At 1200 the 29th Infantry Bde. after a strong enemy opposition gained their objective and occupied the Namah ridge. The situation became quiet and at 1800 the demonstration patrols of 10th and 9th Regts. were withdrawn. Casualties in the Bde. for the day's operations had been nil.

Dec. 28.

At 0600 strong patrols pushed out and at 1100 discovered Khurbetha Ibn Harith clear of enemy. Small enemy posts were located at Kh El Meidan. The country over which the Bde. were now operationg was extremely high, rough and rocky and transport difficulties were increased. Camels were used and found to be very unsatisfactory over the high and rocky hills, and very slow in movement ; their feet were cut on the rocks and their further use off the tracks was forbidden. Improvised roads were made in places and wheeled transport was able to be brought forward to Units Headquarters. Parties from the local villages assisted in this work, receiving from 3 to 7 P.T. per day, according to working capacity. There was little enemy activity with the exception of occasional sniping throughout the day and night.

Dec. 29.

At 0615 10th Light Horse Regt. and 9th Light Horse Regiments moved forward to occupy main defensive line — Khubetha Ibn Harith—Jurdeh, and were in position at 0930. B.H.Q. was established with 8th L.H. Regt. in reserve in rear of Khubetha Ibn Harith. The weather was now settled and fine. Throughout the night 29/30th Dec. there was no enemy rifle or machine gun fire.

Dec. 30.

The relief of the Brigade by the 29th Infantry Brigade commenced at 0900 but owing to the steep and rocky nature of the country was not completed until 1600.

At 2000 the Brigade was concentrated in the vicinity of Kefr Rut. Instructions were received that the withdrawal of the Bde. to Katra would commence at 1100 on 2nd January, 1918, and that the Brigade led horses would reach Bde. Headquarters at 1000 that day.

Since the 27th October, 1917,, the Brigade had been engaged in continuous operations with the enemy, which period was only punctuted with 2 short periods of rest at adi Sucerier, and Mejdel. Considering the severity and number of actions in which the Brigade had been engaged the casualties suffered, with the exception of those suffered from enemy aeroplane bombing, had been extremely light. The health of the troops, with the exception of the epedemic of diarrhoea in 8th Light Horse Regiment had been good throughout. All ranks had been called upon for long periods of endurance and had responded on all occasions.

The Brigade left the hills on 2nd January, and arrived at Belah on 8th January, after a cold, wet and muddy march.

From 8th January, 1918, to 1st April, the Brigade was camped at Belah. The re-organisation and re-equipping was commenced at once, and on 21st January a programme of winter training was commenced—the mounted use of the bayonet, (as a sword), receiving special attention. The afternoons were reserved for recreation, and athletic and mounted sports training, in preparation for the Brigade and Divisional Sports Meeting held on 2nd and 9th March respectively.

Several days were given to rehearsal parades for the review of the Division, mounted, by His Royal Highness the Duke of Connaught, which took place at Belah on 14th March.

Throughout January, February, and March, the Brigade was engaged in salvage operations in the old trenches south of Gaza.

1st April.

On 1st April,, the Australian Mounted Division moved to Gaza en route Selmeh, bivouacing at Gaza, Mejdel, wadi Sucreir nd Deiran, and concentrated at Selmeh, on 5th April.

Preliminary orders for the intended infantry attack and cavalary raid on the Turkish coastal positions, ,(Tabsor defences,) were received, ,nd all preparations by the Brigade were made. The idea was that our infantry should make a gap in the enemy's entrenched line north of Ras El.Ain, and Mejdel Yaba, and that the Australian Mounted Division should push through the gap so made and get behind the enemy line and then operate against his rear, while the infantry carried on against his flank, then opened up by making of the gap. While at Belah the Division had had several rehearsals of the operation, using the old Turkish trenches near Gaza for the purpose. Practise in the rapid cutting and removal of wire, the filling in and ramping of trenches and the rapid passing of defiles by cavalry had been there practiced also.

Reconnaissance by all Officers with special missions in the initial stages of the attack were carried out by day and night, but on 11th April information was received that operations were postponed indefinitely.

April 19.

The 3rd A.L.H. Brigade left Selmeh on 19th April and marched to Taalat Ed Dum, bivouacing at Deiran, Latron, and Enab, and arrived at Taalat Ed Dum on the afternoon of 22nd April. This march brought the Brigade through more mountainous country and steeper roads than had previously been experienced, but the transport overcame all difficulties. The harder road conditions were at once made evident by the increased work for all farriers, and at the end of the march, all horses were extremely shin sore.

The Brigade moved into the Jordan Valley on 24th April, and bivouaced on the open ground a mile north-west of Jericho. The extreme heat was at once felt by the troops and horses. There was now a large concentration of mounted troops in this area, and units were bivouced in scattered formation to minimise casualties in the event of enemy air raids which were now frequent. Parties of officers from the Brigade reconnoitred the country south-east and east of Ghoraniyeh bridge over the River Jordan, (held by 1st and 2nd Brigades), and the defences along the north of the Wadi Auja, (held by N.Z. Brigade and Imperial Camel Corps Brigade). On 26th April 8th Light Horse Regiment moved to high ground to maintain communication with I.C.C. Brigade on the right and left flank of the 53rd Infantry Division at Nejmeh. Preparations were now being made for the operations by the Desert Mounted Corps east of the Jordan.

At the end of April the situation on our army right flank was as follows:— In the previous month-March, a combined Cavalry and Infantry force had crossed the Jordan at Ghoraniyeh, proceeded via the road passing Shunet Nimrin and occupied Es Salt. From there Anzac Mounted Division had pushed on to the neighbourhood of Amman, and a squadron of the 5th Regiment had destroyed a bridge on the Hedjaz Railway, north of that place. The New Zealanders cut the railway to the south of the town. The weather, however, was so bad and the country so boggy that the Mounted force near Amman could not do much so they returned to Es Salt, and the whole force retired west of the Jordan, exclusive of a bridge head at Ghoraniyeh. Prior to this last expedition the enemy line had been Amman Es Salt—Jisr Ed Damieh. He now occupied a strong position at Shunet Nimrin, with about 5,000 men and about 40 guns. They also held a light line across the Jordan Valley from Shunet Nimrin to the left of their forces entrenched opposite Musallabeh. There is only one road from Shunet Nimrin to the enemy bases at Es Salt and Amman, that could carry wheels, any other exists, whether north, east or south were only tracks over which animals could walk with difficulty. The plan of operations of 29th April to 5th May was to attack Shunet Nimrin position in front with infantry and at the same time operate on their rear with the mounted forces. If the Shunet Nimrin road was cut and held, the enemy if they wanted to, could not take a wheel or gun from their advanced position at Shunet Nimrin, nor could their personnel escape, with the exception of stragglers; these would think twice before breaking away over the mountain tracks, owing to the fear of being murdered by the local Arabs. In accordance with this plan, on the night of 29th April, an infantry force of about 4,000 to 5,000 moved over the Jordan by the Ghoraniyeh bridge and attacked the Shunet Nimrin position.

The role of the Desert Mounted Corps was to envelope the right of the enemy's main forces about Shunet Nimrin, capture Es Salt and advance line to Kusr, (142. T. 9,, point 2900, (142.0.35).

The role of the Australian Mounted Division was to advance rapidly northwards east of the Jordan, place one Brigade facing north-west at the junction of the Um Esh Shert—Jisr Ed Damieh and the Es Salt—Jesr Ed Damieh tracks, and block any enemy reinforcements from moving from west to east of Jordan by the Jisr Ed Damieh ford, and the remainder of the Division move on Es Salt from the west and north west. When Es Salt was captured dispositions to be made to protect it from the north. One Brigade to move on point 2900, on the Es Salt—Amman road, (142.0.35), and a detachment to move towards Shunet Nimrin. To the 4th A.L.H. Brigade was given the duty of getting astride the Jesr Ed Damieh tracks. To the 3rd A.L.H. Brigade was given the duty of moving in close support of the 4th A.L.H.

Brigade until that Brigade had gained its above mentioned objective, and then to sieze the entrance to the hills on the Es Salt—Jesr Ed Damieh track, and then to move on Es Salt as rapidly as possible. The 5th Mounted Brigade was to move on Es Salt via the track No. 13 which left the valley near Umm Esh Shert. The 3rd A.L.H. Brigade left it's bivouac near Es Sultan at 2130 on the night of 29th April for the point of concentration on the east side of the Jordan about 3 miles north of Ghoraniyeh bridge. As part of the route to be taken by the Brigade was reported as being unfit for wheels, no wheels of any sort accompanied this formation. Extra pack horses were made available for ammunition and signalling equipment. Each man carried 230 rounds of ammunition, for each Hotchkiss rifle there was 3,100 rounds, and for each Vickers maxim there was 5,000 rounds. In lieu of the Notts battery which was detached to the 4th A.L.H. Brigade, the Hong Kong and Singapore battery, six 12 pounders carried on camels was attached to this Brigade. Their camel ammunition column accompanied them—about 360 camels with battery in column. In lieu of the ordinary ambulance wheeled transport, 29 camel cacholets accompanied the Brigade. The Brigade duly arrived at the point of concentration at about 0145 on 30th April, where it halted for $1\frac{1}{2}$ hours. Whilst there, word was received from the G.O.C., 4th Brigade that he would move ot 0315. This he did. His Brigade moved in line of troop column at extended intervals and distances, northwards up the valley at the trot. As the 3rd Brigade had no opposition to expect unless the 4th Brigade was held up it moved in column of sections, with distances between columns. I considered this the safest formation, as all fire to be expected would come from the flank, and it would be particularly hard for the enemy to estimate the range in the bad light. This Brigade followed the 4th Brigade at the trot. Certain parts of the track had to be followed at the walk, owing to the broken state of the ground but where practicable the pace was at the trot. About $1\frac{1}{2}$ miles south of Red Hill the enemy opened on the Brigade with artillery, and shortly afterwards they also opened with machine guns, whose range, however, was extreme, and their fire did no harm. The fire of the artillery and machine guns continued until the Brigade arrived at the point where the Damieh—Es Salt track cuts the northern track from Ghoraniyeh. It was estimated that the enemy employed 8 guns firing both H.E. and shrapnel. This Brigade had no casualties on its march up the valley. The Brigade arrived at the Jesr Ed Damieh—Es Salt track at 0630, where it was formed up. The 9th Light Horse Regiment was detailed as advanced guard, with instructions to picquet the heights as the Brigade, moved up the track towards Es Salt. This track proved to be an indifferent mountain track, impassable to wheeled traffic of any sort, but passable, with difficulty in most places, to horses, packs and camels in single file. For the whole way the track was dominated by hills on either side, and a few determined riflemen or machine guns could hold up a column until action was taken to outflank the holding-up force. The Brigade took the right hand track which branches off to the right at 127.B.12 central. No enemy was observed until the advance guard arrived at the steep ascent about B.19. Here, a scout noticed a saddley horse near the track, creeping up towards the horse he came on a post of 3 men and observed a troop of 15 cavalry some 300 yards further on. The 3-man post was evidently the advanced post of the cavalry troop. 2 of our scouts got to within 25 yards before they were observed. Finally one of the Turks was killed and the other two captured. Our scouts then fired on the Cavalry troop. 6 of these Turks then abandoned their horses and escaped on foot, the remainder escaped on their horses. 2 miles from Es Salt the enemy were found in occupation of a sangared position astride the road. We were now on the edge of the Jebel Jelaad. We had climbed over 4,000 feet in the 10 miles from Jesr Ed Damieh. The valley is over 1,000 feet below sea level, this range and plateau is over 3,000 feet above it. His position consisted of a high ridge about 1,000 yards long. On his right and slightly to his front there was a detached ridge about 1200 yards away, this ridge was held by him. On his left flank there was another detached hill 1400 yards distant, this was also occupied by him. The enemy held these positions with rifles and machine guns. Troops opened with rifles against these three positions, supported by machine guns, without apparent effect. I decided to make a frontal attack on his position, first clearing up his two flank positions. Time was getting on, the camel guns were particularly slow in movement, any flanking movement would have had to be dismounted—horses could not be taken off the track—such dismounted flanking movements are necessarily slow—darkness would have been on us before anything definite had been accomplished. The country was unknown, time was of the greatest importance. I intercepted a wireless from Desert Mounted Corps to Australian Mounted Division that Es Salt must be taken that evening. I sent a squadron of the 9th L.H. Regiment dismounted, against his right flank position. The enemy were cleared out and the position occupied by us. Enfilade fire was now brought on to his main position from this point. One Gun of the Hong Kong and Singapore Battery then opened on his left flank position. Under cover of its fire and our machine guns, a squadron of the 10th L.H. Regiment with two troops of the 9th L.H. Regiment took possession of his left flank position. Under cover of three guns of the Hong Kong and Singapore Battery and twelve machine guns, a dismounted attack on his main position was organised. It was impossible to move against it mounted—as his position was on a steep rocky hill with terraced sides. Before the attack was made I had the 8th L.H. Regiment standing to their horses with instructions that the moment the 9th and 10th L.H. Regiment got into the enemy's position, the 8th L.H. Regiment would, mounted, push along the track, collect any fugitives they could find, press on to Es Salt and hold the roads from Es Salt to Shunet Nimrin and from Es Salt to Amman, where these two roads meet about half a mile south-east of Es Salt. The attacking troops, two squadrons of the 10th L.H. Regt. on the right and five troops of the 9th L.H. Regt. on the left, formed up in three lines on the ridge about six hundred yards in front of the enemy's position. Five minutes heavy fire from the three available guns and twelve machine guns were opened at the enemy. At the end of that time I gave the signal to advance. The guns and machine guns opened up rapid fire, the stormers (under Major Timperley, 10th L.H. Regt.) sprang forward down the steep rocky slopes and up a similar slope towards the enemy, the conformation of the ground thus presenting an unusually favourable opportunity for covering fire, allowing the men to get within fifteen to twenty yards before it ceased. Many of the enemy bolted to the rear as the assaulting troops neared them, but a good number, amongst whom were German Officers and men, fought till the last and were bayoneted on the spot. The attack with the bayonet was successful—28 prisoners being taken, a number of whom were Germans. As the assault troops arrived on the crest of the enemy position, I ordered the 8th Regt. to advance. This they did at the gallop. I may state from this point on to Es Salt the track was much better as we were now on the plateau. The ridge behind the Turkish position, was occupied an from this the enemy opened a brisk rifle fire. This the 8th Regiment ignored. A little further on, a party of 50 or 60 Turks in sangars were met. A troop was at once despatched to get behind them and the enemy fled. The Regiment then gallopped on to Es Salt. Es Salt was entered at 1830. A German Staff Officer, (afterwards captured), who spoke English was endeavouring to organise resistance in the streets. This Staff Officer afterwards explained that 50 men were sent out from Es Salt early in the afternoon to reinforce the Turkish position, but they failed to arrive. He, the Staff Officer, then took out a squadron which arrived just as our attack was being made. This squadron refused to stop. Subsequently he tried to rally them in the streets of Es Salt, but our advanced regiment rode them down, passed through the town and occupied the junction of the Es Salt, Shunet Nimrin and Amman roads. I would here place on record the very excellent work done by 2/Lieut. Charles Foulkes-Taylor, 10th L.H. Regt., attached to 8th L.H. Regiment. This Officer was in charge of the advanced troop of the 8th L.H. Regt. on entering Es Salt. This Officer raced up to the German Staff Officer, above mentioned, who was then trying to rally his men, demanded his surrender, and told him to stop his men. The German Officer surrendered. Lieut. Taylor took his mauser pistol, he had previously used 14 rounds from his own automatic, emptied two clips of the German's pistol into the retreating enemy and then smashed the pistol over the head of another. The men of Lieut. Taylor's troop were using their bayonets as swords. One sergeant got two on the point, (sword in line). The general opinion was that they were not good for melée fighting—too blunt. They used them for striking. Swords would have been invaluable here. The men with revolvers—Hotchkiss gunners

—were using them freely. The streets and roads were full of mounted and dismounted enemy, 300 cavalry and 200 infantry, the latter escaping in motor lorries and limbers. A large motor lorry full of enemy was escaping along the Amman road, firing as they went. Lieut. Taylor's troop raced after this lorry and stopped it. Two limbers were also seen escaping along the road, one of the drivers was shot and the two teams forced off the road, rolling down a 20 or 30 foot bank. Lieut. Taylor then pursued the retreating enemy a distance of 2 miles along the Amman road, collecting prisoners as he went. He could go no further than this as the enemy put up an organised resistance with machine guns, and Lieut. Taylor had only five men left. It was not possible for more of the Regiment to have been up in time to assist Lieut. Taylor, as it was only practicable to pass through the town in single file. This rapid pursuit was the means of capturing a further 200 prisoners. The 8th Light Horse Regt., for the night, took up a position covering the junction of he Shunet Nimrin and Amman roads. The 9th Regiment was detailed to provide the outpost line protecting Es Salt from the north east to the north-west.

The original divisional instructions were that when two Brigades reached Es Salt the senior Officer would send one Regiment along the Amman road to point 2900, about 7 miles, to cover the track which leads from the south and cuts the Es Salt-Amman road near that point. The 5th Mounted Brigade had not yet arrived, but I considered it important that the above point should be secured as early as possible, as that is a track that fugitives, (if any), from Shunet Nimrin would take.

Accordingly as soon as it was moonlight—about 2200—two squadrons of the 10th Regiment and 4 machine guns under Major Olden, were ordered to proceed to point 2900, (0.30), to block the track from Ain Es Sir where it joins the Es Salt-Amman road at that point. These two squadrons were held up 2,000 yards short of their objective by a Turkish force. Enemy infantry and cavalry were observed in position, local inhabitants stated that Djemal Pasha was in Suweileh with a body guard of 300 Circassian cavalry, and some infantry. Our two squadrons were far too few in number to attack the enemy positions, so remained in position, exchanging rifle an machine gun fire with the enemy and patrolling to the flanks. This detachment kept touch for some time with Brigade Headquarters at Es Salt by telephone, per wire laid by our signallers and by the Turkish wire but both these means were cut by some unauthorised person.

1st May.

The following day when the 2nd Light Horse Brigade arrived, the enemy were attacked by the 5th Regiment and our two squadrons. The enemy retired and point 2900 was occupied by our forces. No further matters of interest developed until the afternoon of the next day, 1st May, when information was received that the 4th Light Horse Brigade had been forced to withdraw about 6 miles from their position, north of the Wai EsSidr, to a line near to wadi El Abyad, and that several columns of enemy had been observed entering the foothills by the Jisr Ed Damieh-Es Salt track. Earlier in the day the Division had ordered me to support the 2nd Brigade at point 2900. At the time that news of the Turkish advance from Jisr Ed Damieh was received, the 8th Regiment and 4 machine guns were moving to the point 2900 to support the 2nd Brigade and the two squadrons of the 10th Regiment and four machine guns there were moving back to Brigade Headquarters. Two troops of the 3rd Squadron of the 10th Regiment were on escort and guard duty in Es Salt. I had thus only two troops of the 10th Regiment available to despatch westwards to occupy a position on the Ed Damieh track and to hold up the advance of the Turks from that direction these two troops were at once despatched. Shortly afterwards instructions were issued by Division that the 2nd Brigade and the 8th Regiment should retire from point 2900, the 8th Regiment to rejoin this Brigade and one squadron to remain on the Amman road, 4 miles from Es Salt. One of the 10th Squadrons under Major Hamlin was there. At 2100 the first of the two squadrons sent to point 2900, rejoined the Brigade. It was immediately sent out to reinforce the two troops on the Ed Damieh track. About 0200 on the 2nd May the 8th Regiment returned to Brigade Headquarters.

May 2.

Information was received from the Commanding Officer, 10th Light Horse Regt., that the Turks were attacking his line and reinforcements consisting of one sub-section of machine guns and one squadron of the 8th Regt. were sent to assist him, also one troop of the 10th Regt. The C.O. of the 10th Regiment had placed a post of about a troop a mile down from the crest line. The Turks, before dawn, attacked this post and outflanked it on both sides. The O.C. of the post accordingly withdrew to the main position on the crest line.

Later on in the morning of the 2nd May, instructions were received from Division that I was to send a Regiment and 4 machine guns to co-operate with the 2nd Brigade against the expected attack from the direction of Amman. I accordingly despatched Major Shannon, D.S.O., with two squadrons of the 8th Regiment, four machine guns and two guns of Hong-Kong and Singapore Battery, and instructed him to collect the squadron of the 10th Regiment, Major Hamlin and his four machine guns on the Amman road on arrival. Major Shannon found that Major Hamlin's squadron and 4 guns, 3rd A.M.Gs. had been in action with the enemy all the morning, holding up the enemy's patrols and advance parties. Major Hamlin's position was in some low foot-hills, 1,000 yards in front of the main ridge running north and south, half a mile east of the first part of the Amman road which runs north. Major Shannon instructed him to retire to the main position occupied by the 8th Regiment. This he did without any casualties.

During the afternoon of the 2nd May the enemy were seen to be thickening up their part of their line in front of the 10th Regiment's position across the Jisr Ed Damieh track. At 1530 they commenced to shell and kept up a continuous fire while their infantry worked up the hills, by dusk their advanced troops were within 100 yards of our line, and they were still climbing the steep terraced slopes. The 10th Regt. on their part had not been idle, sagars of stone, machine gun and hotchkiss gun positions were constructed, ammunition, bombs and flares brought up. As Light Horse Rgts. only carry a few had grenades, (Mills), a plentiful supply of German stick bombs captured at Es Salt were brought up on pack horses and all ranks rapidly made acquainted with their use.

At 2000 the enemy launched an attack against the line held by the 10th Regiment across the Jisr Ed Damieh track. The enemy got within 20 yards on the right and about 200 yards on the left centre, when he was driven back by rifle and Hotchkiss fire. At 2030 he attacked again, but was again repulsed. Except for desultory rifle fire all was quiet until 0200, when he launched a most determined attack, getting to within 100 yards on the left and centre, and 15 yards on the right. This attack was stopped by fire, but the enemy held his position under the rocky ledges and terraces with which the country abounds. At 0400 he again attacked. The right flank of the 10th Regiment was reinforced with a troop and the enemy was driven back with great loss. Our men followed him down with bombs and stones.

About 150 dead were counted in front of the position and there were probably a good number further down the hill. A few prisoners were also taken. The enemy retired to a position about 1,000 yards west of our line, where they remained during the 3rd and 4th May. These last named operations and those hereafter mentioned against the 9th Light Horse Regiment at Kefr Huda, to the right, are those, no doubt, referred to by Djemal Pasha in his reports to his Commander-in-Chief where, in para. 3, he states that "the Turkish 66th Infantry Regiment had come to a complete standstill at noon on the 3rd May, and encountered energetic resistance '; also in Von Papen's report, where he says (para. 1), that, "These heights are covered with the dead of the the 66th infantry regiment."

That afternoon Division re-allotted the outpost lines, the 2nd Brigade was to take the line from El Awab, north to the Amman road inclusive. The 3rd Brigade from that point through Kafr Huda south-west and southerly to the junction with the first Brigade about H34. The 3rd Brigade was to detach to the second Brigade two squadron and 4 machine guns. Major Hamlin, with his squadron of the 10th Regiment was to return to the Brigade reserve. That evening prisoners were taken in the neighbourhood of the 8th Regiment's left flank, near the Amman road, who stated that the enemy intended to attack there early next morning, and accordingly Major Hamlin was instructed to remain at the Amman Road and connect up with the 9th Regiment.

The 8th Regiment (Major Shannon, D.S.O.), less one squadron, and plus one squadron of the 10th Regiment, was placed under the orders of the 2nd Brigade and held a line Kh El Fokan, (J21), through point J.15d.8.2., and along the ridge of high ground running north to J9d88. A force of the enemy advanced to within 800 yards of this position and remained hidden in dead ground and high grass all day. At dawn the following morning, 3rd May, the enemy advanced to the attack. During the night he had crept up close in the long grass. The attack was launched against the whole front of the 8th Regt. A squadron of the 5th Regiment rendered valuable assistance with cross fire from the right. The enemy attacking the right squadron were driven back into the dead ground. The firing died away about 0630 and Major Walker, who was in charge of the left squadron of the 8th Regiment reported that the enemy were then lying in dead ground within 30 yards of his position. Two machine guns were placed in such a position that they enfiladed the ground in front of the squadron, and it was owing to this that the enemy could not retire, they having passed inside the zone of fire during the darkness. A troop was then sent round their flank. When this troop appeared in the enemy's rear, the whole of them surrendered—319 in all, including several Germans and a battalion Commander. A further enemy force was then observed advancing along the same route as that taken by the first and halted in the dead ground above-mentioned. They were still in this position when we withdrew at dusk under orders for the general retirement. During the action two guns of the Hong-Kong and Singapore Battery rendered valuable assistance.

On the morning, 3rd May, the Turks made a determined attack on two of our posts on the Kefr Huda ridge. The post near Kefr Huda was attacked by fifty or sixty Turkish infantry well supplied with grenades. Our post consisted of 2/Lieut. Masson, one sergeant, one corporal and 12 other ranks. The Turks got to within 15 yards of the post before the post retired. By that time 2/Lieut. Masson had been wounded, his corporal and 1 other killed, and 5 wounded (including his sergeant-, and the Hotchkiss rifle destroyed by bombs. The survivors of the post retired to an adjoining post. The Turks then endeavoured to advance along the ridge, but were held up Shortly afterwards, from 200 to 300 Turkish infantry were seen in the captured position. The question of counter-attacking to recover the lost post was considered, but was postponed until a decision had been arrived at as to whether the general outpost line should not be shortened, and thereby strengthened. A fresh column of 3000 enemy infanry had now arrived from the west of Kefr Huda and further bodies of Turkish troops could be seen moving west, along the Amman road. The extended outpost line as then held, had been quite safe for the first 2 days that it was in position. The tactical situation was, however, now altering owing to the large enemy reinforcements which had arrived and were further likely to arrive. The Brigade had no troops in hand to support the front line if a break occurred. I accordingly recommended to the Divisional Commander that our front line fall back on to the line held by the infantry when they occupied Es Salt in March last. This would shorten the Brigade line by half and bring our line back 2,000 yards south of Kefr Huda. Kefr Huda did not appear to me of any special tactical importance. The enemy could not bring wheeled artillery into that locality. As an observation post it was of no use to observe the Shunet Nimrin road. The Divisional Commander approved of my suggestion and orders were issued by me for the necessary withdrawal. Before same, however, could be effected, orders were issued for the retirement of the whole of the force at Es Salt.

The infantry that had attacked the Shunet Nimrin position from the valley had not made much headway and the Turks refused to attempt to evacuate their strong position. The force sent down the Shunet Nimrin road from Es Salt by the 5th Mounted Brigade did not put any appreciable pressure on the rear of the enemy infantry position. The enemy infantry at Shunet Nimrin refused to surrender or run. On the other hand, the enemy forces around Es Salt were becoming hourly stronger. There was only 1 mountain track, (No. 13), still open for the retirement of several mounted Brigades. The track itself was threatened. If the enemy could push the 4th Brigade another mile down the valley, or push the 1st Brigade off the ridge, covering that track on the north-west, that means of return to the valley would be closed. It would have been remained for the mounted forces in the hills to re-open one of these tracks by force, or to march south-east of Shunet Nimrin position and gain the Jordan valley, just north oh the Dead Sea.

As soon as it was dark the 8th Regt. rejoined B.H.Q., half mile north-west of Es Salt. The 9th Regt. was ordered to retire to a position immediately north of Es Salt and remain there until midnight 3/4th May, covering the tracks northwards from Es Salt, the Regiment then to retire by track No. 13. This Regiment left out small parties on its original outpost line until 2330, where they kept up a desultory fire. They then fell back on to their Regiment and the Regiment retired by No. 13 track without interference, passing through the 2nd Light Horse Brigade, at 0130, on the No. 13 track. The 10th Regiment was ordered to retire from the left flank in a southerly direction until they struck the No. 13 track. This they did in conjunction with the 3rd Regiment, which was holding a position on their left flank. The 10th Regiment left out small parties on their original outpost line until 0030. About an hour before they finally left, the enemy made several mild attacks along their front, apparently feeling to see whether the positions were still occupied. They were met, however, with Mills bombs, rifle grenades, and rifle fire, and did not press the matter. At 0430 the Regiment moved on to the Umm Shert, (No. 13) track, and moved in rear of the 2nd Light Horse Brigade and in due course reported to Brigade in the valley.

The Brigade, (less 9th and 10th Regiments), moved from Es Salt at 1945, and got on to No. 13 track and moved on to the position without further special incident. It there came under the orders of the Anzac Mounted Division. The Brigade remained during the day, as Anzac Divisional reserve about a mile east of the Auja crossing. From there it moved back to its bivouac near Es Sultan at 1900, arriving at the latter place at 2200 on the 4th May. On the Brigade's arrival in the valley on the morning of the 4th, the 8th Regiment and one section 3rd A.M.G. Squadron had been sent north along the foothills to reinforce the 4th A.L.H. Brigade and remained there holding a portion of the line until that Brigade retired at 1900. The 8th Regiment arrived at its bivouac at 0300, on the 5th.

The weather during these operations was excellent. It was cool and pleasant, with the exception of one morning with a light drizzling rain, it was dry.

The Brigade moved off from Jericho with 3 days food for men and 14 lbs. forage for horses, no further supplies were issued to us in the hills. This meant that the men were without rations on the 3rd instant. This difficulty was got over by requisitioning half pound meat per man. There was plenty of stock in the vicinity of Es Salt. No forage was issued for the horses on the 2nd and 3rd instant. This difficulty was got over by local grazing which was very good, and by seizure of enemy grain at Es Salt—oats, barley, wheat and maize. Aeroplanes dropped several packages of bandages and stores for hospital patients. The wounded had a bad time when being brought back to the valley. The only conveyances were camel cacholets. They are uncomfortable at any time,, but coming down No. 13 track on the night 3/4th, they were particularly so, as the track was steep, (a drop of over 4,000 feet in 10 miles), and covered with loose stones so that the animals frequently stumbled and sometimes fell.

Attached herewith is a list of prisoners and military stores captured by the Brigade during these operations :—

PRISONERS.

	Gemans.		Turks.	
	Off.	O/R	Off.	O/R
In Hospital Es Salt.	—	—	—	95
Captured in field (unwounded)	1	43	26	541
,, ,, ,, (wounded)	1.	4	—	50
Enemy personnel in hospital .	—	1	2	27
Totals	2	48	28	713

MILITARY STORES.

Machine guns	28	
Automatic rifles	7	
Motor lorries (Bergmann).	5	
Motor Cars (Presto). ..	1	
Motor Cycle	1	
Motor ambulance (Adalem)	1	
Numerous quantities M.G. parts and spare parts.		
M.G. Ammunition, Boxes..	500	
M.G. water cans	100	
Ammunition, 4.2 Howitzers	650	rounds.
„ 10 c/m gun..	120	„
„ 75 m/m F gun	1120	„

Stick grenades	2500	
Ball, match grenades ..	78	cases.
Light waggons	6	
Small cart	1	
Water cart	1	
Barbed wire	100	coils.
Barbed wire standards, wooden	1500	
Bell tents	6	
Fantasis	10	
Tallow	40	tins.
Grain, mixed	1300	bushels.

The following is a list of Brigade casualties during these operations :—

Unit.	Killed.		Wounded.		Missing.		Wounded & Missing.	
	Off.	O/R	Off.	O/R	Off.	O/R	Off.	O/R
B.H.Q.	—	—	—	.1	—	—	—	—
8th L.H.	2	3	2	23	—	—	—	—
9th L.H.	1	4	3	15	—	1	—	1
10th L.H.	—	8	4	18	—	—	—	—
3rd M.G.S.	—	2	1	5	—	—	—	—
3rd L.H. F.A.	—	—	—	1	—	—	—	—
Total	3	17	10	63	—	1	—	1

Total Casualties 95.

The appearance of mounted troops at Es Salt came as a great surprise to the enemy. From conversations with prisoners and a Turkish staff officer, who surrendered later at Damascus, but who was with Djemel Pasha at Es Salt a few minutes prior to our arrival there, it appears they considered the tracks used by us as impassable to mounted troops. They knew there was a movement on. From their positions at El Haud, with good glasses they could observe the slightest movements in our lines. They knew the advance had started, on the night of the 29th, as the head lights of scores of our motor ambulances were observed after dark moving from Jericho to Ghoraniyeh. The enemy expected the attack at Shunet Nimrin position only. This Staff Officer informed us that the IV. Army lost seven Staff Officers, that evening— five killed and two captured. A captured German Staff Officer, one of the two captured, remarked with reference to the charge, into Es Salt on the evening of the 30th, that we galloped our horses where no one else would think of riding at all. He had good reasons for his surprise as the tracks were steep and rocky and the streets of Es Salt were paved with smooth and slippery cobble stones. At the capture of the Turkish Headquarters at Nazareth on October various documents were captured, amongst them copies of correspondence with reference to the operations, between the Commander-in-Chief, Field Marshal Limon Von Sanders, Major Von Papen, the Chief of Staff of the IV. Turkish Army, and Djemel Pasha, the Commander of that Army, which was then occupying Es Salt. Copy of correspondence is annexed hereto Appendix " G." The Higher Command was very satisped with the work done by this Brigade during these— the Es Salt—operations. The Divisional Commander, Major-General H. W. Hodgson, C.B., C.V.O., in an official report dealing with these operations, to Desert Mounted Corps, stated :—"The work of the 3rd Light Horse Brigade was brilliant in the extreme."

That the enemy appreciated the Brigade's action in these operations is evidenced by an intercepted wireless report of theirs, which stated that "Es Salt was captured by he reckless and dashing gallantry of he Australian Cavalry.'

REFERENCE MAP, PALESTINE 1/63360.

On the afternoon of the 4th May, when the mounted troops retired west of Jordan and into the Ghoraniyeh bridge head, the Auckland Mounted Rifles were left on the east bank of the river at the Auja ford, as it was intended to form another bridgehead there. A pontoon bridge was then thrown over the Jordan, 100 yards south fo the ford.

May 5.

Next day, the 3rd A.L.H. Brigade moved to the River Jordan at Auja ford. The 9th and 10th Regts. with 3rd M.G. Squadron, relieved the Auckland Mounted Rifles Regiment in the Auja bridgehead defences.

8th Light Horse Regiment watched the country between the river Jordan and the Wadi Mellahah, and provided working parties for wiring the bridgehead defences.

By day, strong mounted reconnoitring parties were sent out through the scrub to get as near as possible to the foothills east-north-east and north and maintain a line of defence. These encountered enemy patrols throughout each day, but enemy patrols usually maintained a defensive attitude and sniped.

The enemy shelled our defences intermittently day and night with H.E. and shrapnel.

Every available man in the Brigade was now day or night digging and wiring a bridgehead defence to the El Auja crossing.

No unusual enemy movement or activity was observed but our defences were frequetly shelled. Enemy aeroplanes ere active daily over the Auja bridgehead and a great deal of shrapnel and nose caps from A.A. guns fell amongst the Brigade regularly.

The exceptionally dusty conditions which now prevailed in the valley rendered observation difficult, but increased enemy activity on their defensives at and between Tel El Nimrin and Red Hill was detected. Snipers concealed in the scrub were very active and casualties for men and horses of our patrols occurred. Prisoners were captured daily. From these it was found that the enemy water transport arrangements in the Jordan valley area were bad, and the Turks came down to the stream to draw water during the night. Special patrols were sent out to watch for this and capture enemy parties.

May 21.

On 21st May enemy planes bombed our lines but our casualties only slight, a short trench alongside bivouac of each man had been dug when the Brigade first occupied the area.

June 2.

At 0530, 2nd June, the enemy with 10 machines carried out a severe bombing raid and heavy casualties to horses, mules and donkeys were suffered, but by immediate occupation of the short trenches, comparatively light casualties to personnel. The casualties in the Brigade were :—Personnel, 10 other ranks. Animals, 103.

The heat of the Jordan valley had now become intense and the dusty conditions were very trying. Cases of malaria began to appear.

During this period of garrison of the Auja bridgehead, a great amount of work was carried out and the defenses were considerably improved and strengthened. Close contact with the enemy was maintained day and night. Much valuable informaiton of the enemy was gained and many prisoners taken by our patrols.

June 4.

On the 4th June command of No. 1 sub-sector, (Auja Bridgehead defenses), passed from G.O.C., 3rd A.L.H. Bde. to G.O.C., 22nd Mounted Bde. and the 3rd A.L.H. Brigade withdrew to No. 4 sub-sector with headquarters at Ain Ed Duk.

9th L.H. Regiment, 1st section, 3rd A.M.G.S., relieved the garrison of No. 4 sub-sector, (Wood, Wild, Wain, Wart and Wax posts), from 7th A.L.H. Regiment (2nd Brigade), at 2030 4th June, and 8th L.H. Regiment with two sections 3rd M.G.S. were placed at disposal G.O.C. No. 3 sub-sector, to enable the work at centres of resistance on the Bluff-Abu Tellul line to be pushed on rapidly.

Patrols were sent out at irregular intervals throughout each day to Tel El Truny to patrol north and east from there; enemy patrols were encountered, but these always retired to the sangars and small trenches on prominent points near Tel El Richer and Tel El Musseterah, when fired on by our patrols. From Tel El Truny any enemy movement towards Wadi Auja could be seen and the enemy was kept under close observation.

The improvement and strengthening of the defences of the "W" posts was carried on by night.

June 11.

On 11th June an Officer's patrol gained touch with the right of the infantry at Nejmeh after a very rough climb.

The enemy in front of No. 4 sub-sector showed little activity and remained concealed in the trenches and behind the sangars.

June 15.

10th A.L.H. Regiment were ordered to Ghoraniyeh bridgehead on 15th June to remain in support in connection with minor operations being carried out in that sector, and N.Z.M.R. Brigade relieved the 3rd A.L.H. Brigade as garrison to No. 4 sub-sector.

The 3rd A.L.H. Brigade moved to Wadi Kelt, to be prepared to move to Ghoraniyeh at 15 minutes warning.

On completion of these operations on night of 17th June the Brigade left the Jordan valley and its dust and heat for Talaat Ed Dumm en route to Solomon's Pools, where a rest in the cool hills was enjoyed until 10th July.

The severe climate conditions of the valley had raised the percentage of sick of the Brigade very much. Numbers had already been evacuated with malaria.

Reference map Palestine, 1/63360.

July 10.

On the evening of the 10th July the Brigade marched to Talaat Ed Dumm with a view to relieve on the night of 16th July the 1st A.L.H. Bde. as garrison of No. 3 sub-sector, (Musallabeh), of the line.

At dawn on 14th July, orders were received to march at once to the forward area —the enemy had lauched an attack on Musallabeh and Abu Tellul positions in No. 3 sub-sector. On arrival of the Bde. at Jericho at 10-30 information was received that the counter-attack by 1st A.L.H. Bde. had broken up the enemy attack and that all lost positions had been regained.

9th Light Horse Regt. moved to support the N.Z.M.R. Bde. who were to operate on the left of the line at No. 3 sub-sector, but at 2100 returned to Wadi Nueiameh, 1¼ miles N.E. of Jericho and bivouaced with the remainder of the Brigade, without having been engaged.

The attack had been made by 1400 Germans and two Divisions of Turkish infantry on the line held by the 1st Brigade and the 5th Regiment of the 2nd Brigade. The two Turkish Divisions on the right of their attack were completely repulsed—part cf the German force broke through the line between two strong points. Those who got through were counter-attacked by the 3rd A.L.H. Regiment and all were either captured or killed. The Germans opposite the 5th Regiment were repulsed, then counter-attacked with serious loss to the Germans. 500 prisoners in all were taken, including 350 Germans. A subsequently captured document refers to "the unfortunate attack on the Auja, where the Germans and Turks each lost 600 men."

The relief of the 1st A.L.H. Brigade from No. 3 sub-sector was carried out during the night 15/16th July. Throughout 15th July the whole of the area was heavily shelled and heavy casualties had been sustained by 1st A.L.H. Brigade in men and horses, particularly the latter.

Our horse lines, bivouacs, and watering places were within range of the enemy batteries—some of them were with in direct view of the enemy observation posts, and even if they could not see them in the folds of the ground they had no doubt where they were, as the horses had to go to water twice a day. Their planes were frequently over and, no doubt, took photographs of our camps. As the horses had practically no cover from shell fire it was then decided that the whole of the horses, less those of the reserve Regiment with detachment of Machine Gun Squadron bivouaced behind the steep Madhbeh ridge, would be sent back to the Wadi Nueiameh and thus out of range of anything less than 5.9.

8th L.H. Regiment with one section 3rd M.G. Squadron were on right of sub-sector—Muskerah, Musallabeh, and 10th Light Horse Regiment on the left Vise, Vale, View, Vaux, Zeiss and Zerum posts.

There was little enemy rifle or machine gun fire, but enemy artillery was active day and night and there were a few casualties.

The heat and dust of the Jordan Valley, (1,000 feet below sea level), was most unpleasant, and temperature from 110 to 122 degrees were recorded. There was a plentiful supply of water in the area from the Auja stream, although continually under enemy shell fire. The horses that were in the area had to be watered in this stream and often drew enemy shelling.

All available men in the Brigade were employed in digging and the improvement and wiring of the defenses. The night working parties were continually shelled.

Active night patrolling was carried out in front of all positions but enemy always moved back quickly when encountered. The enemy endeavoured to reconnoitre our positions regularly, especially Musallabeh.

The large number of men sent to hospital with malaria caused concern. Anti-mosquito work had been carried out daily ever since the troops moved into the valley. The work consisted of draining all stagnant pools where practicable, if not, putting oil on them; with regard to running streams, reducing their width by filling in with stones and so making them flow faster and by blocking all side back waters, where water could become stationary. This action was taken with respect to all water under our control, but unfortunately a large part of the stagnant water in the district lay between the two lines and the enemy fired on all parties, working thereat. Practically every Officer or man that patrolled over this swampy land, though it was on one night only or who occupied one of the posts on the edge of the swamp, contracted malaria.

Men on sentry wore mosquito gloves and a net but without much avail, a net under such conditions is little protection.

The specially organised system of day and night observation was carried out and no enemy movement passed unobserved.

The enemy was in strength at Baghalat, with advanced positions along Grant ridge from which he sniped. Guns shelling the Brigade were located at Um Es Shert, Red Hill, (large calibre), Wadi Fusril and Chalk Ridge.

The situation remained the same except for a lively bombing encounter on the early morning of 6th August between enemy patrols and ours.

The enemy was noticed preparing defensive positions on left bank and head of the Wadi Mellahah, linking up with their Bag Halat system. On nights of 8th and 9th August special patrols of 1 Officer and 6 men from the 9th Regiment were sent to reconnoitre these. To reach these positions it was necessary to avoid and get behind the enemy patrols between Grant Ridge and Wadi Mellahah. These were worked round and our patrols discovered that the enemy manned these positions in strength at night.

On 10th August No. 4 sub-sector was added to command of G.O.C., 3rd A.L.H. Brigade. 1st Battalion, B.W. Indian Regiment took over the garrison from 9th and 10th Regiments in F and G sections on night 13th August.

9th Regiment to Ain Ed Duk and 10th Regiment to cover of high ground S.W. of Madhbeh ridge as supports and 8th A.L.H. Regiment as sector reserve.

The relief of the sub-sector caused increased movement in the area and enemy artillery was active day and night. Mussalabeh received special attention from enemy guns, but the trenches and dugouts of this position were so prepared that artillery effect was very slight.

The troops had been called upon for continuous night digging as well as for the garrisoning of the defences. The dust and heat was still great (temperatures averaging from 108 to 117). From casualties and sickness the strength of all units of the Brigade was now considerably reduced.

Aug. 22.

G.O.C., 1st A.L.H. Brigade assumed command of No. 3 and 4 sub-sectors on night of 22nd August and on completion of relief 3rd A.L.H. Brigade marched to Talaat Ed Dumm en route Ludd, where the Australian Mounted Division concentrated.

The Brigade arrived at Ludd on 26th August and camped among the olive groves there. Reinforcements, (but not sufficient to bring the Units up to establishment), came forward. Equipment was got up to date and swords, the long straight cavalry pointing pattern, were issued to all ranks. The cavalry or double rank drill was adopted; Major Cavanagh the G.S.O. 2 of the Division put a class of Officers through sword drill, these Officers then became the instructors of the troops. Two imperial cavalry sergeant instructors were borrowed from the Training Centre Moascar, and these assisted in the instruction. The instruction which the Brigade had received at Belah during the previous February and March in the use of the bayonet as a sword now bore fruit. After a few lessons the men were passed by the Imperial Instructors as quite competent to operate against Turkish cavalry. Troops were exercised in shock tactics with rapid detachment of machine guns and Hotchkiss Rifle to the flank. Up to now we had always carried 230 rounds of ammunition on the men; in view of the issue of swords this was now reduced to 180, 90 in the bandolier on the man and 90 in a second bandolier on his horse. Intensive training was carried out throughout the Brigade until 18th September.

On the evening of 18th September, 1918, the Turkish 7th and 8th Armies held an entrenched line from Tabsor on the coast to a point on the Jordan about 10 miles north of Jericho. The 4th Turkish army held the hills commanding the Jordan Valley east of the River. It was the intention of the Commander-in-Chief to concentrate a superior force of Infantry on the coastal sector, break the line there, and push three of the four cavalry Divisions through the gap to the rear of the Turkish forces. This cavalry force was to then, capture or destroy the Turkish armies south of the line Damascus—Beirut. The fourth available cavalry division, (Australian and New Zealand Mounted Division), with four infantry battalions, one Indian infantry Brigade and certain artillery—all known as Chaytor's Force, were to operate in the Jordan Valley against the 4th Turkish army based on Es Salt and the Hejaz Railway. The Australian Mounted Division was to pass through the gap in the rear of the 4th and 5th Cavalry Divisions, and follow the 4th Cavalry Division in close support as far as El Lejjun and then operate as the exigencies of the situation required.

Sept. 18.

After a three weeks period of intensive training the Brigade marched on the evening of 18th September to a bivouac site near Selmeh in preparation for the offensive which was to commence at dawn on 19th September.

Sept. 19.

At 0902 on 19th September the Brigade left the bivouac and marched 6 miles per hour to Jelil crossing the Auja River at Yellow House Bridge. Horses were watered at Jelil and the Brigade moved 2 miles east to a position of readiness to await orders to cross the enemy trench system northwards. At 1100 a Despatch Rider on his was from Corps to Division was intercepted. He was carrying orders for an immediate move forward for the Division, so in anticipation of instructions the Brigade moved off following the route taken by the 4th Cavalry Division passing the battlefield where Richard the 1st of England signally defeated Saladin in 119:.

This route led through Tabsor—Kh Ez Zerkie— El Mughair—to Esh Sh. Muhammed on the Iskanderun River where the Brigade arrived at 1930 and watered. Advice was received from D.H.Q. that the Brigade would probably move on for El Lejjun at 0100. The 19th Brigade R.H.A. had so far been attached.

Sept. 20.

About 0130 on 20th September the Brigade moved on for Lejjun the remainder of the Division following. A well defined track was followed as far as Zelefeh after which the direction was changed to the north-east across country. 10th L.H. Regiment formed the advance guard. Beidus was reached at 0700, prisoners and material captured by the 4th Cavalry Division being passed on the way. The Brigade pressed on through the hills and through the Musmus pass along the good road to Lejjun, following the same track as that taken by Thotmes III of Egypt, when he in 1479 B.C. moved to attack the King of Kedesh at Megiddo, (Tel El Mutesellim). El Lejjun was reached by the vanguard at 0945. Brigade watered and fed and sent out observation posts to the north and one troop along the Jenin road to remain in observation on the high ground about Salin. Brigade had thus marched 51 miles in less than 25 hours. A halt of several hours now took place pending receipt by Desert Mounted Corps of information as to the situation with regard to the 4th and 5th Cavalry Divisions, particularly as to the situation towards Haifa. The necessary information having come to hand being eminently satisfactory, orders were issued to this Brigade, (less one regiment), to move on Jenin and capture the hostile fugitives reported to be retreating east and north-east from that place. By 1630 the Brigade, (less the 8th L.H. Regiment left for local protection at Lejjun), with Notts battery, R.H.A., attached, was on the move. 10th L.H. Regiment (Lt. Col. K.C.N. Olden) with 6 machine guns were advanced guard, a troop of the 9th Regiment as right flank guard A pace of 10 miles per hour was maintained. Near Tannuk, half way to Jenin, a small enemy outpost was captured by the flank guard. As the advance guard approached Jenin, a large enemy force was observed camped amongst the olive groves, immediately north-east of Kefr Adan The right flank troop of the vanguard under Lieut. Doig immediately charged them with drawn swords. The enemy promptly surrendered. A few minutes afterwards the right flank guard to the main column, (Lieut. Cruddas of the 9th Regiment), arrived on the scene in support of Lieut. Doig, followed shortly afterwards by two more troops of the 9th Regiment, (Lieut. J. M. McDonald), sent out from the main body. These additional troops helped to round up the enemy scattered through the olive groves. The enemy was apparently astounded at the sudden appearance of our men. The captures here amounted to 1800, including many Germans. There were also 400 horses and mules captured. This episode, however, did not delay the general advance of the column. The Brigade pressed on. The advance guard pushed rapidly on leaving the railway station about half a mile on their right so as to get astride the main road leading north and the route leading east to Beisan. The remainder of the Brigade followed at a fast trot in close support. By 1740 the vanguard had reached Jenin, the remainder of the column with guns was close in rear, thus having marched 11 miles in 70 minutes. By 1800 all northern and eastern exits had been closed. Once astride the roads and railways the 10th Regiment turned south and drove back in towards the village and station. By this energetic action the enemy were driven into confusion and our men riding in amongst them with drawn swords made prisoners of about 3,000. It now became dark andpressing on to clear the town our troops were held up by rifle and machine gun fire from a party of Germans concealed in houses and gardens. Later this party tried to break away and there was some confused fighting in the darkness. The Germans were caught by a section of our machine guns, (under Captain Bryant), as they tried to break for the road and a number were killed, they then surrendered without further opposition. Prisoners were collected, troops assembled and dispositions made for the night. The left flank troop of the advance guard, (Lieut. A. W. M. Thompson, M.C.), captured 27 motorlorries near Besneh. A strong patrol of the 9th Regiment was sent north to the vicinity of Mukeibileh, near where they located an abandoned motor convoy of 29 vehicles. The 10th L. H. Regiment moved through the town took up a position across the main road from Nablus, where it comes through the pass about one mile south of Jenin. Lieut. Patterson with his sub-section of M. G. was sent to support them but in the poor light, got ahead of the squadron that they were to join. Some little distance down the Nablus road at about 2100 they saw a large body of enemy approaching in the moonlight—2,800 in fact with 4 guns. The Officer thought it rather a big order for his troop of 23 to take on, but his Corporal, (Lance-Corporal B. George), proferred the advice that it was safer to bluff it out than retire. The Officer agreed. He put a burst of machine gun fire over the heads of the leading troops and called upon them to surrender. At first they demurred. It was their first suspicion that there were any hostile troops in front of them. In fact the Germans afterwards railed against the Turks for the latter's failure to keep them posted as to the situation. But the Turks themselves were equally ignorant. This column now found itself in a narrow gorge, wide enough for the road only, with steep hills on either side, over which single men could climb with difficulty. They were aware that they were being followed from the south. Their advance was blocked by a party of enemy whose strength they could not gauge in the moonlight. Machine gun bullets were whistling over their heads to expedite their decision. There was at the head of the column a German nurse who spoke English fluently. Lieut. Patterson told her that there was an overwhelming force just to his rear. She passed his information on and after a short conference between the enemy leaders, the whole party surrendered. The night passed without further incident, but every available man was employed collecting prisoners and material and in holding the approaches. Over 8,000 prisoners, including many officers of high rank, 5 guns, numerous machine guns, two aeroplane and a vast amount of material and boot of all descriptions had been catpured, including a war chest wagon loaded with gold and silver coin. Much material was burned by the enemy, his dumps and aerodrome with 24 aeroplanes burning fiercely all night. Many of the Turkish and German Officer prisoners admitted being taken completely by surprise at our unexpected appearance at the northern exits of Jenin, stating that they thought we must have landed at Haifa, never believing it possible that we could have made such rapid progress up the coast.

Sept. 21.

At dawn while looking around the outskirts of the town in the neighbourhood of the railway station. The Brigadier, A.D.C., and Orderly came upon a batch of 40 Turkish soldiers and a 10 c.m. gun. The former were waiting quietly to be collected. This was duly done by a few men from the 9th Light Horse Regiment who were sent for.

At 0700 the 8th L.H. Regiment arrived and took charge of the prisoners escorting them back to Lejjun. Guards were posted on captured material and patrols sent out to stop looting by Arabs. The streets of Jenin were blocked with abandoned transport, and their loads and stores were littered about. Much looting had been done by the inhabitants. The 10th L.H. Regiment remained on observation of the approaches to the town from the south, south-east and south-west. The Turkish and German hospitals were full with sick and wounded. Guards were posted here and the cases fit to travel evacuated by lorry. A number of motor vehicles had been captured and these proved useful for collecting material and sick and wounded prisoners. Orders were issued for the 9th L.H. Regiment to send down one squadron via Fukua, to reconnoitre country towards Beisan, and capture small parties of enemy reported to be in that area, and for the 10th L.H. Regiment to send one troop south along the Nablus road to gain touch with the 5th L.H. Brigade. Duringt he day a number of enemy straggles were rounded up and brought in. A and B1 echelons marched in.

Sept. 22.

At dawn the reconnoitring squadron of the 9th L.H. Regiment, (Major Parsons, D.S.O.), moved out through Fukua and swept country to within two miles of Beisan, capturing about 80 prisoners. Our cavalry were observed in that place. While on this reconnaissance Corporal A. H. Todd of A squadron with the right flank patrol, observed a party of 3 officers and 28 other ranks concealed behind a cactus hedge, near the village of Jelbon. After reconnoitring their position, the patrol charged them with drawn swords, upon which the enemy promptly surrendered. The troop of 10th L.H. Regiment, (Lieut. Doig), pushed south along the Nablus road, as far as Ajje, but did not gain touch with the 5th L.H. Brigade. These detachments joined the Brigade later at Afule. At 1330 the Brigade marched off for Afule, with orders to report to the 5th Cavalry Division at that place for instructions. Meanwhile we had been advised that the 8th L.H. Regiment having handed over prisoners at Lejjun, had received direct orders to march to Nazareth, and there relieve a Brigade of the 5th Cavalry Division. Orders from the 5th Cavalry Division were for 1 Regiment, (10th L.H. Regiment), to relieve a Brigade of the 5th Cavalry Division of the line Shutta-Zerin and for one Regiment (9th L.H. Regiment), to take over all guards and duties at Afule. 3rd L.H. Brigade were to be responsible for administration of Afule. 8th L.H. Regiment were in occupation of Nazareth and were responsible for administration there. The Brigade arrived at Afule at 1700, watered and fed. 9th and 10th Regiments then moved out and carried out reliefs as above, all being completed by 0300.

Sept. 23.

Dispositions remained unchanged. Two squadrons of the 10th Regiment were employed in escorting 4,000 prisoners taken by 4th Cavalry Division from Shutta to Afule, where 9th L.H. Regiment provided guards for them. The 10th Regiment pushed a patrol out beyond Tumrah, but found no signs of the enemy. The 8th Regiment and 4 machine guns at Nazareth were disposed so as to cover the Tiberias and Acre roads, and found the necessary picquets and guards in the town to protect the captured material and maintain order. A patrol from this regiment to Kafr Kenna, reported all clear, but refugees stated enemy were in strength at Tiberias.

Sept. 24.

The 8th Regiment pushed out patrols to Ailut, and Beit Lahm, and reported all clear. The 10th Regiment escorted 4,000 more prisoners from Shutta to Afule, after which the Regiment withdrew from the line Shutta-Zerin, which was then taken over by the 5th L.H. Brigade, and came into bivouac near B.H.Qrs. Orders were issued for the 8th Regiment to send one squadron from Nazareth at dawn the next day to reconnoitre Tiberias.

Sept. 25.

"A" squadron of the 8th L.H. Regiment, (Major McPherson, M.C.), left Nazareth at 0500 and moved to reconnoitre Tiberias. A transmitting station from the Brigade Signal Troop, with an escort of one troop of the 10th Regiment, (Lieut. A. B. Gollan), was at the same time despatched to Mt. Tabor, 8 miles north-east of Afule. This hill —1843ft. in height—is the most commanding point in the whole district and through it touch could be kept with any patrol. The squadron lost visual touch with its Regimental Headquarters at Nazareth very shortly after leaving that place. A motor cyclist was attached to the squadron for carrying despatches. Tiberias is about 18 miles north-east of Nazareth, on the western shore of the lake of Tiberias, and about 6 miles north from Semakh, on the extreme southern end of the lake. The main road from Semakh to Damascus runs up the western side of the lake and through Tiberias. The 4th L.H Brigade were to attack Semakh at daylight on the 25th and advance up the western side of the lake. At 0900 the squadron reached Lubieh, and communications were established with the Brigade transmitting station on Mt. Tabor by heliograph. From this point the country was more difficult, and the heights and roads on the left flank had to be picquetted, as it was known that the enemy had considerable forces in the vicinity of Safed. The light armoured motor battery reported to the squadron at Kurn Hattin. The patrols were approaching Hajaret En Nusara, and no resistance had been met with. When the enemy had discovered the presence of our troops on Nusara, which overlooks the town and is about 1500 feet above sea level, patrols were sent by them to try and ascertain our strength. These patrols were soon cut off by our mounted men and captured, and as all natives were prevented from entering the town, the Turks had no information as to the number of our troops in that locality. One troop under

Lieut. J. N. Stubbs, with Hotchkiss Rifle, was sent to point Z8, central, (on the beach, two miles north-west of Tiberias), to prevent the escaping enemy using the main road leading north along the lake. Forward patrols and the armoured cars fired upon machine guns, (known to be 6), from a point just north of the town. Two N.C.O. prisoners reported 200 Turks, 50 Germans and 13 machine guns holding the place. About 150 Turks, 3 motor cars, 2 motor lorries, and a number of horse drawn transport could be seen from Nusara retiring along the beach road, they were fired on by our troops in Z8 central and all retired to Tiberias, motor-cars and lorries being abandoned along the road. At 1130 a squadron from the 4th A.L.H. Brigade reached El Menarah, south of Tiberias, and the O.C. thereof reported to Major McPherson. He made arrangements to attack the town at 1400. The 4th Brigade squadron advanced mounted from the south-west, one troop of the 8th Regiment along the sea shore from the north-west, a second troop of the 8th Regiment was sent from the west with orders to make good the gun positions, 500 yards north of the town. The 4 armoured cars advanced along the main road. Slight resistance was met with from the gun position which was charged by a troop of the 8th Regiment with drawn swords. The enemy abandoned their weapons and fled in disorder over the rocks on to the beach and into the town. No further resistance was offered and 8th Regiment troops at 1500 gallopped on and entered the town from the north simultaneously with the 4th Brigade squadron from the south and the armoured-cars from the west. Large quantities of military stores, motor-cars, motor-lorries, transport and machinery were captured, also 175 Turkish and 25 German prisoners. The signalling station on Mt. Tabor was particularly useful. When the squadron first arrived at Tiberias, it at once reported the situation. This was passed on to Division who then instructed the Brigade to move that evening and attack Tiberias in the morning. Brigade at once signalled Major McPherson to remain in close touch with the enemy as Brigade would be there by the morning. Seeing his opportunity, however, that Officer captured the town with the assistance of the squadron from the 4th Brigade, and at once flashed Brigade the result.

At 1700 the 3rd Brigade marched off for Tiberias, one squadron of the 10th Regiment was away escorting prisoners to Lejjun and the relief of the 9th Regiment at Afule had not yet been completed. Instructions were left for these Units to follow on. Brigade arrived at a point 2 miles west of Tiberias at 0500, and bivouaced. Our left flankers passed over the battlefield of Hattin, where, in 1187, Saladin exterminated the large Crusaders' army under King Guy, which was endeavouring to relieve Tiberias. The 19th Brigade, R.H.A., joined the column at Kefr Kenna, and one troop, 10th L.H. Regiment, which had been escort to visual transmitting station on Mount Tabor, (keeping touch with reconnoitring squadron at Tiberias), joined at Lubieh. At 1015 the Brigade moved to a bivouac at Mejdel, on the western edge of the sea of Balilee. Horses and men bathed in the sea, and were thus much refreshed after the night's long march. Two squadrons of the 8th L.H. Regiment were employed to restore order and guard stores in Tiberias. A reconnaissance of two troops of the 8th L.H. Regt. was pushed along the coast to the village of Tabghah. This place was found all clear and the inhabitants were friendly. They provided plentiful good forage for horses and refreshments for men. One squadron 9th L.H. Regiment left at 1230 to reconnoitre Safed where a considerable force of the enemy had been reported. They reached this point at 1800 and reported all clear. These reconnoitring parties remained out during the night, the squadron at Safed, withdrawig to the main road, near the Jewish village of Rosh-Pina. There were two machine guns with the squadron. Outposts for the night were established at Kh. Irbid and all lines of approach round the bivouac area.

Sept. 27.

Shortly after midnight orders were received that Division would move at 0600 with the object of relieving Damascus on the 29th instant. At 0730 3rd L.H. Brigade moved off, following 5th L.H. Brigade as far as Rosh Pina, after which the 3rd L.H. Brigade, with 9th L.H. Regiment and 6 machine guns as advance guard, took the lead. It had been reported that the Jordan bridge at Jisr Benat Yakub had been blown up. Orders had therefore been given for the squadron 9th L. H. Regiment at Rosa Pina to push forward at dawn and reconnoite the fords as far as Lake Huleh. The 3rd

Field Troop were pushed on ahead to collect material and repair the bridges. Our orders were to reach the high ground overlooking Kuneitra before dark. At 0930 while on the march a message was received from advanced squadron, 9th L. H. Regiment that the enemy were holding Yakub and the Jordan crossings with machine guns and at least one field gun, and were entrenching. Aeroplane reconnaissance confirmed this—the total enemy force being estimated at 600—800. The Division halted at Rosh Pina, the balance of the 9th L.H. Regiment with Notts Battery, R.H.A. being sent on to clear up the situation. It soon became apparent that the enemy were determined to vigorously dispute the crossing of the river. Lt. Hannaford reported a crossing not held by the enemy about 2 miles south of the bridge, at El Min. The enemy no doubt recognised that every hour he could hold the Division up was of vital importance. His IV. Army was now in full retreat from Deraa towards Damascus. He no doubt hoped that if those 20,000 fugitives could get a little rest at Damascus, he could organize a defence of that place against our purely cavalry force. It was imperative that they should not get that rest and chance to reorganise. The Divisional Commander therefore decided on an immediate general attack. The 5th L. H. Brigade were to cross the river to the south of Yakub bridge at El Min and work round the enemy's flank, while the 3rd Brigade were to engage the enemy in front, and if possible get round his right flank by crossing immediately south of Lake Huleh. The 9th L. H. Regiment moved and engaged the enemy between the lake and the bridge, pinning him to his ground and forcing him to disclose his dispositions and strength. The Notts battery early in the fight silenced the enemy guns, obtaining a direct hit upon one of them, and effectively kept down the fire of enemy machine guns which had been located by the 9th L. H. Regiment. The 3rd M.G.S. took up positions along the western bank from which effective covering fire could be given to troops crossing the river. Vigorous reconnaissances under heavy rifle and machine gun fire for a crossing of the river was carried out by the 10th L. H. Regiment, and a ford was located half a mile south of the southern end of the lake. 8th L. H. Regiment were sent to join the 9th Regiment, the plan being for the 8th and 9th Regiments 3rd Machine Gun Squadron and Notts Battery, R.H.A. to give covering fire while 10th L. H. Regiment crossed. After this Regiment had established itself on the eastern bank, the remainder of the Brigade would cross. It was expected that the operation would be facilitated by the fact that the 5th L. H. Brigade at 1630 were reported to be crossing the river at El Min without opposition and would therefore soon make themselves felt on the enemy's flank. It turned out, however, that the country to the east of the 5th Brigade crossing place was so rough that they were unable to get on to the main road until after daylight next morning. Up to 1700 the enemy hung on to his positions with determination, at times developing considerable rifle and machine gun fire, causing us a few casualties. By 1730 all covering troops were in position and the 10th L. H. Regiment moved forward to cross at the ford previously located, under heavy covering fire from the remainder of the Brigade. The water was about 2'6" in depth. The 10th L. H. Regiment were all across by 1915 and were followed at once by the 8th L. H. Regiment. These two Regiments were directed to make for Deir Es Saras, the 10th L. H. Regiment detaching B squadron to move south along the river to clear up any enemy still in position. This squadron encountered a party of enemy in the dark who opened fire at a few yards range causing casualties. Without hesitation the leading troop under Lieut. M. H. Macnee flung themselves off their horses — it was too rough to charge mounted — and with fixed bayonets rushed the flashes. A sharp fight took place and for a time the enemy fought with great determination inflicting several casualties on us. The balance of the squadron soon supported the leading troop and the enemy surrendered. The post included 12 Germans, 41 Turks, 1 field gun and one machine gun, and one motor lorry. During these operations it was apparent that the enemy were extensively using motor lorries as a means of withdrawing the troops, comprising their rear guard on this sector. In the morning a large number of these had been seen moving down to the river positions. Similar tactics were two days later adopted by them at Sasa.

Sept. 28.

The balance of the Brigade followed the 8th and 10th Regiments across the river and after a night march over extremely rough and hilly country, shortly before dawn was collected about Deir Es Saras. The 10th and 8th Regiments reached this place before midnight. An enemy ammunition dump was found here. Horses were watered and fed, and visual communication established with Divisional Headquarters west of the river. Owing to the bridge being broken, all wheels including Notts Battery, R. H. A., had to be left on the western side. At 0600 three enemy aeroplanes the first seen in the air since operations commenced, passed overhead. Aeroplane reconnaissances reported that about 1200 enemy were holding the high ground about Kuneitra. At 0930 the Brigade moved of for this place, the 8th Regiment and 6 machine guns providing the advance guard. Anywhere off the road the country was extremely rough and stoney, and flankers could only move slowly across it. By 1140 the head of the main column had reached Tel Abu Ell Khanzie and the vanguard was climbing the slopes of Tel Abu en Neda which overlooks Kuneitra. Eight Circassion horsemen who had sniped at our scouts were captured here. They were fine looking men, well mounted, and armed to the teeth. Fifty enemy cavalry were seen retiring from Ayun Suaan but Kuneitra was occupied by 1300 without opposition. Horses were watered in the village and at 1600 the Brigade moved on to the vicinity of Jeba and bivouaced for the night. 35 Miles had been covered by the Brigade in 34 hours, some of it over very rough country and in the face of enemy opposition. Except for two hours at Deir El Saras horses had been saddled for the whole of the time.

Sept. 29

At 1500 the Brigade moved off, remainder of the Division following at 1700. The 9th Light Horse Regiment and 6 machine guns were advanced guard. The objective was Damascus in order to cut off the Turkish 4th Army retreating through that place from the south The general situation was that Chaytor's force had on the 27th captured Amman and on the evening of this day — the 29th — captured 4,564 prisoners 20 miles south of Amman, being the southern part of the IV. Turkish Army. Our 4th Cavalry Division and the Sherifian army were pursuing the remainder of the IV Turkish Army northward along the railway towards Damascus. The 5th Cavalry Division was moving in rear and in support of the Austrlian Mounted Division. A reconnaissance in the morning by armoured cars had reported a force of enemy estimated at 300 with machine guns and 2 guns astride the road about 4 miles south of Sasa. One squadron of the 9th Regiment and 2 machine guns were pushed on in advance to reconnoitre enemy's position. The remainder of the Brigade reached the Nahr Mughaniye and there watered. From here it could be seen that enemy were shelling the advance squadron with at least one battery and a report was received that the enemy were in position, and had at least 6 machine guns. It afterwards appeared from statements of Officer prisoners that their strength was 1 company of German machine gunners, about 300 strong, 1,200 Turkish infantry and 4 guns. They considered that they would undoubtedly hold the Division up as they thought it impossible for mounted men to travel anywhere off the road. On one part of the road they had laid 5 machine guns with the centres of their cones of fire 50 yards apart. They were sure that nothing alive could pass through that. Major Parsons, O.C. "B" squadron, 9th Light Horse Regiment reported enemy holding very strong position astride road approximately between Kanikir and about 2½ miles S.W. of Sasa. Earlier in the evening this squadron engaged the enemy to find out his strenght and dispositions of flanks. The enemy were occuping a low chain of hills astride the main road on a frontage of about a mile. On approaching this position over extremely rocky country, "B" squadron came under very heavy machine gun fire and the right flank was cut off. This action had the effect of making the enemy expose the position of his left flank. At 2030 "A" and "C" squadrons, with Major Daly, D.S.O., in charge, moved around the left flank of enemy position with orders to fire a green flare when the hill on extreme left of enemy position was gained and cleared. It was a difficult movement over extremely rough country composed of lava formations with large crevices several feet deep, and the leaders were at a great disadvantage in not having had an opportunity of making a daylight reconnaissance. «B» squadron were ordered to clear the hill nearest the main road on the right of the enemy position and to fire a red flare, when the first crest was clear of the enemy. When the red flare was fired it was found that the enemy were still holding the intervening higher ground on about a mile frontage, and the least movement on the road started heavy enemy machine gun fire, the guns having been laid during the daylight. At 2200 green flares were observed in direction of "A" and "C" squadrons and at 2230 Major Daly reported by telephone that he had gained the ridge on extreme left of enemy position, and "A" squadron were working along ridge. The enemy were too strong for the 9th Regment to deal with and the 10th Light Horse Regiment were sent forward to support the 9th Light Horse Regment by attacking the enemy's right flank. The main strenght of the enemy lay in his machine guns, with which he was able to put a very effective barrage on the road. At 2200 two troops of "C" squadron 10th Light Horse Regiment went forward to get in touch with the 9th Regiment. In doing so they encountered an enemy post on an advanced crest line. This post they captured with one machine gun. Three of the enemy were killed. Lieutenant Gwynne, D.C.M., was here wounded.

Sept. 30.

At 0200 as the 9th and 10th Light Horse Regiments were making only slow progress, 8th Light Horse Regiment, (less, 1 Squadron) was sent in dismounted to storm the enemy position frontally from the road. Co-operation by the 9th and 10th Light Horse Regiments was arranged for as far as darkness time, and the exceedingly rough nature of the ground permitted. By 0300 the 8th Light Horse Regiment had captured the enemy position with five machine guns, and a few German prisoners. During the advance, the Regiment was subjected to a heavy rifle and machine gun fire. The enemy beat a hasty retreat towards Damascus, vigorously pursued along the road by the 10th Light Horse Regiment. The advance was again held up temporarily about one mile south of Sasa. The vanguard with two machine guns attached dismounted and rushed the enemy, who then broke and made off towards Sasa in motorlorries, which had been brought up behind their lines. In the course of this pursuit the 10th Light Horse Regiment captured two 77 M. M. field guns, 2 machine guns, one motor lorry and about 20 prisoners. The Brigade had orders that from dawn onwards the 4th Light Horse Brigade would form the Divisional advance guard, while the 3rd Light Horse Brigade assembled after the action just concluded. Shortly after the 4th Light Horse Brigade took up the pursuit they overtook and captured several hundred fugitives. At 0645 all troops of the Brigade had reached Sasa, and at 0730 the Brigade marched following the remainder of the Division. On arrival at Khan Esh Shiha, Divisional orders for the approach on Damascus were received. The 5th Light Horse Brigade, closely followed by the 3rd Light Horse Brigade were to outflank the town by moving via Katana, north easterly along the foothills of Kalabat El Mezze. Bourchier's force, (two Regiments of 4th Light Horse Brigade), were to move directly on the town via Daraya. Soon after this movement commenced enemy machine gun fire was heard directed against Bouchier's force from the vicinity of Kaukab. The 19th Brigade, R. H. A. engaged these machine guns, the 5th and 3rd Brigades meantime pressing on to their objective at the trot. When a point half a mile north of Mudhamiye had been reached, troops of Bourchier's force, were observed galloping the enemy's position, supported by the fire of the R. H. A. batteries. Away to the east could be seen shrapnel bursting, no doubt from the artillery of the 14th Brigade of the 5th Cavalry Division sent across to intercept the Turkish third cavalry division retreating on Damascus. The 5th and 3rd Brigades pressed on, until at a point about 1½ miles south west of El Mezze the French Cavalry Regiment which was leading was held up by machine gun fire from the garden west of the southern end of the town. The R. H. A. batteries were brought up and engaged these machine guns — the 3rd Light Horse Brigade remaining halted ready to support the 5th L. H. Brigade when and where required. The enemy machine guns concealed in the gardens were difficult to locate and swept the open ground over which any direct advance would have to be made. About 1530 orders were received that the 5th L. H. Brigade were to turn into the hills on their left and cut the road and railway leading north west to Beirut along which the main line of retreat of enemy troops in Damascus lay, while the 3rd L. H. Brigade, were to make their way to the N. E. road leading to Homs and Aleppo and block that line of retreat. The Brigade at once moved off, 9th Light Horse Regiment and 6 machine guns forming the advance guard. After a short advance over rough hilly country the Brigade reached a point about 1 mile S. W. of the village of Dumar. Reconnaissances soon showed that the nature of the terrain was such that an advance across country over Jebel Kasiun was impossible. The only alternative was the main road from Dumar through Er Rabue and then through the northern end of Damascus itself. In preparation of this the leading squadron of the 9th Light Horse Regiment and four machine guns took up a position on the high ground immediately S. W. of Dumar. Large bodies of the enemy were seen to be retreating along the road from Damascus to Beirut. They were in a closely formed column of infantry, transport and guns. This column was caught at effective range by the fire of our rifles and machine guns. Those who had passed before our occupation of the high ground commanding the road above Dumar were caught by the fire of the 5th Light Horse Brigade further to the west, while still further west again a squadron of the 8th Light Horse Regiment was also in position commanding road and railway. It is estimated that at least 700 casualties were inflicted on the enemy in this gorge of the Barada, in addition hundreds of animals were killed; horses, cattle, donkeys, sheep and dogs. The remainder of the column lost heart and returned back to Damascus and no doubt formed the bulk of the 12,000 prisoners who were collected there next morning. The Beirut road was thus closed at sunset on 30th September. A visual station had been sent out to get communication with Division and through it orders were now received for the Brigade to bivouac in its present position for the night and march for the Homs road at 0500 the next day in pursuit of enemy retreating to the north east. Loud explosions were heard in Damascus, and the flames of burning stores lit up the skies throughout the night.

The 9th Light Horse Regiment and 6 machine guns remained all night in position above Dumar sweeping the roads by fire and preventing any escape along this route by the enemy. Such targets are more dreamed of than realised by machine gunners.

At 1910 two troops of the 9th Regiment, (Lieutenents Hargrave, MC and Lieutenent Masson), reconnoitred the village of Dumar and found same clear of enemy, except for dead sick and wounded and a few stragglers. The main road to Damascus was packed with transport but with little trouble would be passable to mounted troops. The bridges over the Barada were intact. A Turkish guard was still on sentry at the railway station.

Not with standing rough country and the delaying action fought by the enemy southof Sasa, the Brigade had covered 34 miles in 26 hours without off saddling, except for one hour at Sasa.

1st Oct.

The situation in Damascus at this time, it was afterwards ascertained, was as follows: Djemel Pasha, Commander of the Turkish IV Army arranged to hold a meeting of the Notables of Damascus at the Municipal Gardens at 4 p.m., on 30th September, 1918, for the purpose of handing over to Shukri Pasha Ayoubi the Military Governorship of the City. The last mentioned person was an Arab, formerly in the Turkish army and favourable to the Sheriff of Mecca. There was in the city at this time a person of Algerian birth named Emir Said. This man had been for some time past employed by the Turkish Government in raising a volunteer force of Arabs to fight against the Sheriff. Emir Said's sympathies were really in favor of the Sheriff, but he had disguised the fact and drew arms, and ammunition and money from the Turks.

Some time prior to 2 p.m. on the 30th news was received in the city that the British Cavalry were approaching. A report was also circulated in the city that the Germans intended to burn the city before they left. Shukri Pasha Ayoubi and Emir Said then went to Djemel Pasha and informed him that they would not allow the city to be burned and advised Djemel Pasha to leave the city forthwith and stated that if he would not, he would be attacked by the local Arabs.

In Djemel Pasha's presence these produced the Sheriff's flag, displayed it on the Town Hall, and declared for the Sheriff, Djemel Pasha then, at 2 p.m., left the city by the Beirut Road.

By 0500 this Brigade was on the move, the 10th Light Horse Regiment (Lieutenent Colonel Todd, D. S. O.), forming the advance guard, with Major L. C. Timperly (C Squadron) commanding the Vanguard. The column descended to the main road at Dumar and moved along it south easterly into Damascus. Some delay was caused by the road being blocked by enemy transport and animals the result of our machine gun fire the night before. The head of the enemy column had been utterly overwhelmed, dead and wounded strewed the road and filled the houses on either side. In one place a flock of sheep which had evidently been accompanying the column had all been killed and a dog attempting to cross the road had perished. At Dumar station a train with troops aboard was captured. 483 prisoners were taken here together with fifteen machine guns, two 77m.m. field guns, ,and large amount of gold and silver coin, and further along the road six more guns and fifteen machine guns were found abandoned. On entering the north-west suburbs a good deal of rifle shooting was indulged in by the inhabitants. Some of the shooting was sniping at the column. In a few cases the snipers were observed and the fire was returned. To discourage the sniping the vanguard moved on at the gallop, until it arrived in front of the Town Hall, where it halted. The time was now between 0630 and 0700. Major A. C. N. Olden, Second in Command of the 10th Regiment was up with the vanguard. Accompanied by Major Timperley, he entered the Town Hall. A large assembly of notables and people in uniform was in attendance. The civil Governor was asked for. Emir Said came forward and said:—" In the name of the civil population of Damascus I welcome the British Army" and then made a speech of welcome. A guide to the North-East or Aleppo Road was asked for. Emir Said detailed an Officer called Zeki Bey to act as such. This Officer stopped with the Brigade until the following morning but was more inclined to parade the column throught the streets of Damascus than expedite our pursuit of the enemy along the Homs Road, so that shortly afterwards the offer of an English speaking resident of Jaffa, Mr. D. N. Tadros to guide us through the intricate and narrow streets of the city to the north-east was gladly accepted. This gentleman had been exiled from Jaffa some time previously by Djemel Pasha owing to the formers English sympathies.

The advance guard then moved on, followed on by the remainder of the Brigade, passed through the city and moved on to the North-East road passing the English Hospital en route.

The 3rd A. L. H. Brigade were thus the first Allied Troops to enter Damascus. I understand that it has appeared in the press that the Sherifian forces were the first to enter. This is not so. His force had been moving up from Deraa with the 4th Cavalry Division, Col. Lawrence, of the Sherifian Army, with an escort pushed on to Damascus on the morning of the 1st October and were seen to enter the city a few minutes before 0800. By that time this Brigade had come and gone. As there were none of our troops left in the city at 0800, the absence of any British troops may have given rise in the minds of the Sherifians to the erroneous belief that they were the first to enter the city. Up to the time, (about 0700), that this Brigade completed its passage through the city thereby closing the only available exit for the enemy, no member of the Sheriff's army was visible in any part of the city within view of this Brigade.

As the main body of the Brigade marched through large numbers of the enemy were observed on our right about the Government Buildings and the Baramkie Barracks. They showed no signs of opposition or hostility. All lines of retreat were closed to them; moreover it was essential that this Brigade should gain the Homs road and press on in pursuit of the enemy retreating along it with all speed possible. The enemy in the town was therefore passed by and left to be dealt with later. Eventually it was reported that the 4th L. H. Brigade had collected upwards of 12,000 there. As the Brigade passed through the streets the crowd gave vent to loud acclamations and every sign of joy, and distributed flowers and fruit amongst the troops. When the advance guard reached the north-east outskirts, information was received that the Bridge over the Wadi Maraba was held by Germans with machine guns. The 10th L. H. Regiment pressed on and cleared up the situation by dismounted action, taking 12 prisoners and 2 machine guns. As the advance guard approached Duma the enemy again brought machine guns into action. One squadron of the 10th Regiment, however, most ably assisted by four machine guns under the command of Lieut. Patterson worked round and attacked the enemy's right flank with fine dash, capturing 500 prisoners, (including 40 Germans and 37 machine guns). The enemy made another stand at Khan Kussier but again were vigorously routed after some street fighting, in which our machine guns, (6), under Captain Bryant, took very prominent part. 40 Germans, 120 Turks and more machine guns being taken. The country from Damascus to a mile past Khan Kussier is denseley covered with vineyards and olive groves, admirably adapted for rear-guard action with machine guns. The enemy tactics appeared to be to fight the machine guns in a rear guard action to the last moment, and then to abandon them and ride off to the next position, bringing fresh guns into position there. From Khan Kussier about 2,000 enemy cavalry and infantry were seen heading for the pass into the hills north of Khan Ayash. The enemy had now reached the plain and were extended across it on a mile frontage across the road. They were here again aiding the retreat by the use of machine guns, which they would bring into action a few at a time, and if necessary abandon. They mounted two guns in a house about a mile from the pass but abandoned one complete and the mountings of the other, but not before they had done their work. A large portion of their force was mounted but our machine guns kept in action at ranges from 1,000 to 1,500 yards by frequently pushing on. Attempts were made by mounted attack to cut off the enemy from the pass. A squadron of the 9th Regiment was sent up on the left under the foothills to cut him off, but heavy and skilfully directed machine gun fire from guns already in position held them up. The hills on the left were impassable. The whole of the 9th and 10th Regiments and the machine guns squadron were now engaged, the rear of the enemy column was being pressed across the open country between Khan Kussier and Kubbet I Asafur. At this stage the C.O., 10th Regiment, received a report from his right flank patrol that a force of some 3,000 cavalry was moving towards us from the north-east and then about 4 miles away. This occasioned me much concern. Some of the machine guns were down to their last belt. Their limbers could not possibly join up for hours. A force of 3,000 mounted men within half an hour of my flank had to be considered. The 10th Regiment accordingly ceased the pursuit and was got in hand. A strong squadron of the 8th Regiment together with the Brigade Scouts were sent out to the right to reconnoitre the reported cavalry. In due course they reported that it was an enormous camel convoy consisting of thousands of camels with armed riders, being the big annual caravan from Aleppo to Mecca; they caused us no further anxiety, but in the meantime the enemy whom we had been pursuing were safe in the hills. During the day's fighting amongst the olive groves and vineyards north of Damascus and across the open land towards the hills the Brigade had taken 744 more prisoners and 80 machine guns. The Nott's Battery had not accompanied us on this day's march, being left in the valley near El Mezze, being unable to accompany us over the hills towards Dumar on the Beirut Road. We were also unfortunate with our Field Ambulance. Without reference to the Brigade it had been stopped some miles to the south-west of Damascus, and put on to the job of collecting sick and wounded Germans and Turks. The result was that we had not even a stretcher to give our men wounded on the 1st of October. Wounded men were carried in to bivouac on the front of horses and later on in two delapidated buggies, which we seized locally for the purpose—some ambulance wagons turned up in the afternoon of the 2nd October, after my strong remonstance that I thought the Brigade's wounded should have first call on it's own ambulance.

    As the last feed issued had been eaten at dawn, and as the Brigade had as yet had no time to requisition for more, it was necessary to return to Duma to draw feed by requisition. The Brigade bivouaced for the night about two miles north of the village, orders being issued for a strong patrol of the 8th Regiment to push out along the road towards the foot hills at dawn and for each of the Regiments to put out an outpost line to protect their bivouac from the east.

Oct. 2.

Shortly after 0600 a local inhabitant reported to B.H.Q. that there was a party of two hundred Turks asleep five kilos to the east of our camp. Instructions were at once sent to the 8th Regiment (with four machine guns) to go and collect them. Before the 8th Regiment had left it's lines, however, (it was bivouaced about a mile towards Damascus) the night outpost of the 9th Regiment (the forward Regiment) observed at 0615 a column of infantry moving north, one mile east of Regimental bivouac. The Regiment at once saddled up. Brigade was asked if it were known who they were, Brigade replied that believed to be enemy and to move out at once and investigate, and that the 8th Regiment and four machine guns would support. It will be remembered that the 8th Regiment and four machine guns had been warned some time previously to move out. The 9th Regiment moved at 0645. It was apparent that the enemy column were making for the pass, where the Aleppo road enters the hills at Kubbet I Asafur. The 9th Regiment had tried to intercept the enemy there the previous afternoon, so knew exactly what to do and the country over which they would be required to pass. The remainder of the Brigade was ordered to saddle up and follow. The Brigadier and Staff went by motor-car along the Aleppo Road. The 9th Regiment moved out at a gallop. It was imperative that they should get to the pass before the enemy could occupy it with machine guns and hold us off. The Regiment then pushed along the road for half a mile, then left it and swung to the left under the foothills. At this time the rear of the enemy column was about one mile head on the main road. The Regiment soon gained on the column which had now mounted several machine guns and pushed out small left flank guards. Although the Regiment came under rifle and machine gun fire, its pace was not checked and it soon reached a favorable position about 1 mile from left flank and opposite the centre of the enemy column. "A" squadron then raced for Khan Ayash and "C" squadron for Khubbet I Asafur. The remaining squadron, "B," dismounted and opened fire on the centre of the column with a view to throwing it into disorder. By 0735 the two leading squadrons had got level with the cavalry advanced guard of the column and was swinging on to the main road. The head of the enemy column now appeared to be in a state of uncertainty and their leaders appeared to be conferring. Simultaneous with the final movement of the two advanced squadrons, the remainder of the Regiment drew swords and charged the main column. The combined movement was entirely successful. The main column surrendered before our troops reached them, and the Hotchkiss rifles which were covering this advance were ordered to cease fire. "A" and "C" squadrons, with drawn swords, quickly charged the enemy advanced troops, composed mostly of cavalry. "A" squadron at Khan Ayash rushed a machine gun just as it was mounted and ready to fire. "C" squadron seized the pass and captured two 7.5 e.c. guns near Khubbet I Asafur. The whole enemy force amounting to 91 Officers, 318 cavalry, 1064 infantry, 8 Germans, 26 machine guns, 1 mountain gun, 2—7.5 c.m.—CKN guns, 12 automatic rifles, 285 animals were captured within one hour of Regiment moving from bivouac at Khan Kussier, approximately 7 miles.

Amongst the Officers captured was the Divisional Commander who defended Shunet Nimrin against our attacks in May, 1918. The Regimental Standard of the 46th Regiment was captured. Personnel captured belonged mostly to the 46th Regiment.

When main column surrendered signaller J. M. Smythe and signaller M. C. Halliday were moving back to Regimental Headquarters Signal Station when they encountered a party of the enemy composed of 3 Germans and 85 Turks, taking up a position within a few hundred yards of the signal station. A German Officer was mounting an automatic rifle, when Smythe and Halliday with great gallantry rushed the German Officer, taking his pistol, fired into the enemy, and seized the automatic rifle. The enemy were so surprised that they surrendered in a body. Both these signallers were awarded the D.C.M.

Our force only suffered one casualty in this engagement.

The casualties in killed and wounded for the final offensive, (19th September to 31st October), were extraordinarily light, viz:—3 other ranks killed and 5 Officers and 23 other ranks wounded. This was in a way balanced by the high rate of sickness.

The 10th A. L. H. Regiment was left on observation in the foothills and a post of 1 troop was left on the Wadi Maraba track. The remainder of the Brigade returned to bivouac near Duma.

VETERINARY.

The horses stood the severe strain imposed upon them very well. The following is the wastage.

19th September to 2nd October.

Killed and destroyed in action ..			25
Wounded ..			15
DESTROYED :—	Exhaustion ..	3	
	Broken legs ..	3	7
	Colic ..	1	
DIED :—	Biliary fever..	1	
	Colic ..	1	4
	Exhaustion ..	2	
MISSING ..			

Transferred to 8th Mobile Vet. Section.

Lame and injuries (kicks) ..	54	
Colic and diarrhoea ..	10	
Laminitis ..	15	
Wounded ..	7	150
Exhaustion ..	22	
Fever ..	7	
Sore backs ..	32	
Sore withers ..	3	
Total..		207

PRISONERS CAPTURED. 20th September to 2nd October.

Date.	Place.	Number.
20/9/'18	Jenin	8107
26/9/'18	Tiberias	100
27/9/'18	Yacub	52
29/9/'18	El Kuneitre	29
,,	Sasa	29
1/10/'18	Er Rabue station	483
,,	Duma	583
,,	Kussier	161
2/10/'18	Kubbet I Asafur	1481
	Total ..	11025

GUNS AND MACHINE GUNS. 20th September to 2nd October.

Date.	Place.	Number.	Description.
30/9/'18.	Sasa	7	Mach. guns.
”	”	2	77 m/m. fld. guns
20/9/'18	Jenin	1	10 c/m. gun.
”	”	5	77 m/m. guns.
”	”	45	Mach. guns.
”	”	4	Auto. rifles.
1/10/'18	Er Rabue station	4	77 m/m. guns.
”	”	2	Mount. guns.
”	”	2	Howitzers.
”	”	30	Mach. guns.
”	Duma	50	” ”
”	Khan Kussier	30	” ”
2/10/'18	Kosh Metwal Chiftlik	3	Mount. guns.
”	Khan Ayash	2	77 m/m. fld. guns
”	” ”	1	Mount. guns.
”	” ”	26	Mach. guns.
”	” ”	12	Auto. rifles.
	Total Guns	22	
	Total Machine Guns	188	

Amongst the vast amount of stores, transport and material of all descriptions captured, was a large quantity of gold, and silver bullion, (estimated at £200,000), and a great quantity of Turkish Treasury Notes. These were all handed in to Division.

EXPENDITURE OF S.A.A. AMMUNITION, 103,000 Rounds.

Oct. 3.

On 3rd October Brigade bivouaced in the vicinity of Duma and moved to south-west of El Mezze on 5th October. One squadron 9th Light Horse Regiment was left at Duma to watch Homs road and other approaches to Damascus. While on this duty they collected 3 more mountain guns abandoned by the enemy. 10th Light Horse Regiment less two squadrons, with 2 squadrons of 8th Light Horse Regiment moved to Kaukab and took over guard of over 16,000 prisoners.

The condition of these prisoners when taken over by us was lamentable. Prior to capture they had been marching for same 10 days—a beaten army. Their supply system had of course, at once, broken down—they were practically starved. They had been closely pursued by the British cavalry, continually bombed by our aeroplanes, and hard pressed by the local Arabs. As soon as these last saw how things were going they swarmed in for loot and revenge. Stragglers, or small detached parties of the fugitives were attacked and usually killed. The result of this stress was that the fugitives were physically and mentally exhausted—3,000 of them were sick. When we took them over they were in a mob under some scattered palm trees near Kaukab on the bank of a creek. They had no cover even for the sick. There were a large number of Officers with them but they were also in a dazed condition and would not make the slightest effort to organise, or ameliorate the condition of the men. Few of the men had blankets, they had no medical organisation. There were no drugs, bandages, or food fit for sick men, no sanitation. Food for the prisoners was scarce. Men were dying at the rate of 170 a day. Lieut.-Colonel Todd took the control of the compound in hand and soon put a different complexion on the matter. Very little assistance could be obtained from the local Arab authorities of Damascus, how had taken possession of the Turkish Army Stores. They demurred from doing anything, unless paid exorbitant rates in gold. They did not like English paper money. However, by bluff and threats, blankets for the men were got out of them, sheep were requisitioned from the surrounding country. Prisoners were organised into companies of 100 each under their own N.C.O's, arrangements were made for the daily cleaning of the area, 3 Syrian Doctors were obtained from amongst the prisoners, the worst of the sick were removed under cover in a neighboring village, and the daily death rate was reduced from 170 to 15. About 1500 died during the period that we controlled the camp. About a week after we took over, Lieut.-Col. Todd started to reduce the numbers by daily convoys of 1,000 each down the lines of communication, via the north of the sea of Galilee. These parties could not go regularly but by the end of the month when we handed over, the camp had been reduced to 3,000 or 4,000.

The remainder of 3rd A. L. H. Brigade moved to south of Kaukab on 9th October and bivouaced. The percentage of sick, (chiefly malaria), was alarmingly high, and a number of deaths, (2 diagnosed as cholera), took place.

The medical conveniences at Damascus for the first couple of weeks after our occupation were anything but sufficient. An epidemic of influenza went through the army. Malaria which was in the system of a large number of the members of the Corps after their sojourn in the Jordan Valley developed rapidly. In addition there were 3,000 Turkish and German sick. The Hospitals at Damascus were overflowing when we arrived. The only organisation we had to deal with sick and wounded was the Field Ambulances attached to our Cavalry Brigades. The personnel of these were sick in large numbers. For instance with this Brigade Field Ambulance there should be 6 Medical Officers, there were only 2, one of these was sent to look after a Hospital in Damascus, and the sole survivor was himself very ill, but carried on. The Hospitals were overcrowded, they could take no one but urgent surgical cases, the Ambulances were overcrowded and sick men had to remain in their lines and get such attention as their comrades could give. In the Hospitals and Ambulances patients could not get proper attention, there were few trained orderlies, drugs and invalids' foods were scarce. The local Arab authorities who controlled the local markets and the captured Turkish army stores were the reverse of helpful. They wanted gold for everything they did and at famine price rates. The evacuations from the Units at the time were extremely large. One Brigade evacuated 61% of it's personnel in one week in October, another 58%. Another cavalry Division sent away over 40% of it's personnel in 10 days. Fortunately there were practically no enemy left after the capture of Damascus, so that the above serious losses by sickness did not have any appreciable affect on the campaign.

The Australian Mounted Division remained in readiness to march to Aleppo and support 5th Cavalry Division, who had continued to pursuit of the remants of the Turkish armies, and on 27th October, 1918, the Brigade, less 10th Regiment, marched to Jobar, en route to Aleppo. Homs was reached at 0530 on 1st November, 1918, after 5 consecutive long marches—the final one from Nebk, (50 miles), proving a big test for animal endurance. The marches were governed by the question of water on the track. At 1600 on the 31st October, when the Brigade was in the vicinity of Hasie, information was received from General Headquarters that an armistice with Turkey had been arranged from 1200 that day. The news was received remarkably quietly by all ranks. The march to Homs was continued and the Division again concentrated.

The Division, less the 5th L. H. Brigade marched to Tripoli, this Brigade moving on the 6th November. The 5th L. H. Brigade later moved to Baalbek. While at Tripoli Brigadier-General G. De L. Ryrie, C.B., C.M.G., took over the command of the Division, from Brigadier-General W. Grant, D.S.O., who had been temporarily commanding while Major-General H. W. Hodgson, C.B., C.V.O., was on leave in England. About this time the Divisional Commander Major-General H. W. Hodgson, C.B., C.V.O., took over the Command of Desert Mounted Corps.

On the 12th January 1919, the C.-in-C. General Sir, E. H. H. Allenby, G.C.B., G.C.M.G., inspected and addressed the Brigade at Tripoli. He was most complimentary in his remarks when addressing the troops. When leaving the Parade Ground he said to me "General Wilson, I congratulate you on your magnificent Brigade."

After handing in most of our equipment and disposing of our horses the Brigade left Tripoli by sea for the demobilisation camp at Moascar, the 8th and 9th L. H. Regiment on the 22nd February, and the remainder of the Brigade on 4th March 1919.

          L. C. WILSON, *Brigadier-General,*
          Commanding 3rd Light Horse Brigade.

Zagazig, Egypt,
  1st April 1919.

  NOTE.—In the middle of March while the Brigade was awaiting demobilisation at Moascar, political unrest, including murder of soldiers and Europeans, looting of shops and houses of Greeks and Armenians, tearing up of railways, destruction of railway bridges, telegraph and telephone lines became general throughout Egypt. All Australian troops, (exclusive of 1st and 2nd L.H. Regiments, who had already embarked for Australia), were re-equipped and sent into the disturbed area. The first part of this Brigade left for Zagazig District on the 15th of March and the balance on the 18th March, 1919.

APPENDIX "A".

Brigade Staff and Commanding Officers of Units during period under review.

Brigade Commander	Brig.-General L. C. Wilson, C.M.G., D.S.O.
A.D.C. to G.O.C.	Lieut. H. J. Cattle, D.C.M.
	Lieut. H. R. Hammond.
Brigade Major	Major W. M. Anderson, D.S.O.
	Major W. J. Urquhart.
	Capt. W. M. Lyall, M.C.
Staff Captain	Capt. M. W. Lyall, M.C.
	Lieut. A. S. Barker.
Vet. Officer	Major S. A. Mountjoy.
8th L. H. Regiment	Lieut.-Col. L. C. Maygar, V.C., D.S.O.
	Lieut.-Col. A. M. McLaurin.
	Major H. J. Shannon, D.S.O.
	Lieut.-Col. T. J. Daly, D.S.O.
9th L. H. Regiment	Lieut.-Col. W. H. Scott, C.M.G., D.S.O.
10th L. H. Regiment	Lieut.-Col. T. J. Todd, C.M.G., D.S.O.
	Lieut.-Col. A. C. N. Olden, D.S.O.
3rd M. G. S.	Major C. L. Nicholas.
	Capt. G. H. Bryant.
3rd Sig. Troop	Lieut. W. J. Latham.
	Lieut. W. D. Glanfield.
3rd L. H. Field. Amb.	Lieut. Col. G. E. M. Stuart.
8th Mob. Vet. Sect.	Major H. Worthington.
	Capt. R. N. Wardle.
3rd Field Troop (Engineers)	Lieut. P. H. Harper.
Notts Battery	Major Harrison, M.C.
R.H.A.	Major Fraser McKenzie, D.S.O.
	Capt. Fosbrooke Hobbs, M.C.

APPENDIX "B".

THE SWORD.

The cavalry sword—long thrusting pattern, (about 42 inches in length), was issued to all ranks of the Australian Mounted Division in August, 1918, prior to the final general offensive. The Division had received, while at Belah, in the early part of the year, 1918, a fair amount of training in the use of the bayonet as a sword for mounted shock action. The bayonet was not, however, satisfactory. The grip was not good, the weapon had a very short reach, it was too blunt for melee fighting, and it was a very skilful horseman who could while riding at the gallop put the point of it through a dummy on the ground. The training, however, that the men received in it's use at Belah showed itself when swords were issued at Ludd, with the result that the Cavalry Instructors passed most of the men as sufficiently efficient after a few lessons. The issue of the weapon, I consider, was more than justified. Was it not Napoleon who said that the moral force was to the physical, as 3 is to 1. I consider the sword has a great moral effect both on the man carrying it and on the enemy. One of the chief values of the sword is the spirit of progress that it inculcates in the carrier. He does not allow himself to be bluffed by slight opposition. He rides on feeling that he has a weapon in his hand, and in 19 times out of 20, finds the opposition only a bluff. With mounted rifleman, on the other hand, his only course is to make wide flanking movements to induce the opposition to retire, or to dismount and try to shift it by fire action. This all means time, or uncertainty, which is exactly what the enemy wants.

Then again, dealing with a pursuing force, as we were in the Beersheba—Jerusalem operations in 1917, and the Damascus operations in 1918. There are numerous cases in these operations where the sword would have been, or was, invaluable. Take the operations about Huj in November, 1917. With my late experience I can see what we could have done with the sword there. We were in touch with large bodies of the enemy somewhat disorganised, retreating, but still armed. We had no swords and could only deal with them by fire action. Their line was too broad to outflank. The Regiments engaged them at a distance and where practicable raced in and cut out guns and transport. They inflicted casualties and took prisoners but did nothing really big. If they had had swords I am now confident from my late experiences that they would have made wholesale captures. It is not reasonable to expect mounted riflemen to charge positions mounted. It is only bluff, and if the enemy stood to it the charge could end in failure only. Such bluffs, I know, have come off, but we cannot always expect to be lucky. For instance the 4th A.L.H. Brigade at Beersheba. At Katia, in August, 1916, my regiment, the 5th Light Horse Regiment, charged the Katia Oasis, mounted, with bayonets on rifles, as lances, in two lines, two squadrons in first line, one in second. The rifle under such conditions is very unhandy. In this case there were only a few enemy there when we arrived. At the first Gaza,—27th March, 1917,—the same Regiment, gallopped the cactus hedges at the rear of Gaza, the men firing their rifles from their horses—the mere appearance of the horsemen among the Turkish battalion holding that sector was quite enough. The fire from the horses was not, of course, very effective—swords would have been of the greatest value there.

Now dealing with cases in the recent operations. As the Brigade approached Jenin on the afternoon of 20th September, a party of 1,800 of the enemy were observed on our right front. They were promptly charged with drawn swords and surrendered. If we had had no swords the procedure would have been a careful approach, then probably a fire fight and we could not have got into Jenin that night. Probably the 6,000 extra prisoners that we got would have evaded us, or had time to organise.

Later on the same evening our men galloping up the streets of Jenin demoralised the enemy much more quickly than a dismounted approach with fire would have done. The quickness of it meant practically no casualties to us.

Take the example of the 2nd October north of Damascus where the galloping approach of a Regiment with flashing swords caused the prompt surrender of a whole column of nearly 1500 men, well supplied with machine guns and guns, and who were not taken by surprise, and had been putting up a defence for the last hour. I am confident that if swords had not been in evidence that morning, it would have happened that the leading Regiment would have taken up a position on the flank of the column and opened fire upon them. The enemy would have continued the fire fight with their numerous machine guns and artillery, all the time moving to the pass. Half an hours respite would have enabled them to get there, once there they were safe. We might have inflicted 50 or 100 casualties on them and would have suffered a good few ourselves. The rushing horses and the swords settled it, we had one casualty, they were all casualties.

I do not wish for a moment to say that swords can be used on all occasions, but I do contend that the mere posession of the weapon which he can use while on his horse instills in a man a spirit of the offensive, and that there are occasions, and many of them, where the sword is by far the most effective weapon and then chiefly by its moral effect. It is the duty of the trained leader of mounted men to know when to use the rifle and when the sword.

L. C. WILSON, *Brigadier-General.*

APPENDIX "C".

Casualties of Regiments of the 3rd Light Horse Brigade from incorporation to 31/12/1918.

Unit.	Dead.		Wounded.		Missing.		P. of W.		Total.		Grand Total.
	Off.	O/rs.	Off.	O/rs.	Off.	O/rs.	Off.	O/rs.	Off.	O/rs.	
8th L.H. Regt. ..	32	273	24	379	—	1	—	3	56	656	712
9th L.H. Regt. ..	12	169	22	362	—	—	—	5	34	536	570
10th L.H. Regt. ..	15	213	41	373	—	—	—	—	56	586	642
Total	59	655	87	1114	—	1	—	8	146	1776	1922
Percentage..	85%	45%	—	—	—	—	—	—	211%	114%	134%

NOTE :—The establishment of a Regiment has varied from five hundred and fifty all ranks to five hundred and twenty two and four hundred and seven eight :— Average, say, five hundred, of whom twenty three are Officers.

Other Brigade Casualties.

1st Brigade 1888
2nd Brigade 1620
4th Brigade { Not available as Gallipoli casualties included in other Regiments.

Casualties of A.I.F. Mounted Troops in Egypt, etc.

Dead 2424
Wounded 5304
Missing 6
Prisoners of War .. 93

Prisoners of War of:—
1st, 2nd, 3rd and 4th Light Horse Brigade.

Officers .. .. NIL.
Other ranks .. 40.

APPENDIX "D".

3RD LIGHT HORSE BRIGADE FIELD AMBULANCE.

Summary of Admissions, Evacuations, Discharges, and Deaths, 3rd Light Horse Brigade, from *1st November 1917, to 30th October 1918.*

Month.	Admissions.		Evacuation.		Discharges to Unit.		Deaths.		Remarks.
	Off.	O/rs.	Off.	O/rs.	Off.	O/rs.	Off.	O/rs.	
1917.									
November	3	229	3	229	—	—	—	—	
December	5	111	4	110	—	—	1	1	
1918.									
January	1	72	1	51	—	21	—	—	
February	3	85	3	48	—	36	—	—	
March	3	81	3	54	—	27	—	—	
April	3	107	3	107	—	—	—	—	
May..	11	361	11	359	—	—	—	2	
June..	5	320	5	304	—	16	—	—	
July..	1	232	1	221	—	11	—	—	
August	20	572	20	564	—	8	—	—	
September	12	446	11	343	1	103	—	—	
October	15	425	13	334	2	84	—	2	
Total	82	3041	78	2724	3	306	1	5	

(Signed) G. E. M. STUART, *Lieut.-Colonel.*
C. O. 3rd Aust. Light Horse Field Ambulance.

APPENDIX "E".

RATION SCALES.

Ordinary. When in standing camps.
Mobile. When on march.
Special emergency. Carried on march when on operations, not consumed unless mobile ration not to hand.
Iron. Always carried—but only used on special orders to that effect and when all other sources of supply fail.

ORDINARY RATION SCALE

Meat fresh	12 oz.
or preserved	9 „ Wood lbs. 2.
Bread, or	1 lb.
Biscuit	12 oz.
Bacon	4 „
Jam	3 „
Milk	1½ „
Vegetables, fresh, or	8 „
Dried vegetables	2 „
Potatoes, or onions	4 „
Sugar	3 „
Tea	½ „
Cheese	3 „
Salt	1/100th oz.
Pepper	1/100th „
Mustard	1/100th „
Lime juice when dried vegetables	1/10th gill.
Rum, when ordered by G.O.C.	½ gill.
Cigarettes	2 oz. weekly.
Matches	3 boxes fort-nightly.

EXTRAS :—

Rice	2 oz. 3 times weekly.
Dried fruit	2 „ weekly.
Ortmeal	2 „ 2 times weekly.
Flour	2 „ 2 do.

	Mobile.	Special emergency.	Iron.
Preserved meat	12 oz.	9 oz.	12 oz.
Biscuits	12 „	13 „	16 „
Jam	4 „	3 „	—
Tea	½ „	½ „	½ „
Sugar	3 „	3 „	2 „
Milk	1 „	—	—
Cheese	3 „	—	—

APPENDIX "F".

FORAGE SCALE.

	Ordinary.	Mobile.	Special emergency.
Grain .. lbs.	10	9	9 ½
Fodder .. „	12	6	—
Draught, over 16 hands, extra grain .. „	2	—	—

APPENDIX "G".

Correspondence between Field Marshall Liman Von Sanders, Major Von Papen, Chief of Staff, IVth Turkish Army, and Djemal Pasha, Commander of IV Army.

4/5/18.

His Honour,
Major Von Papen,

I regret to have to inform your Honour that I am not in any way *in agreement* with the various measures recently adopted by the Chief Command of the IV Army.

The VIII Army Corps fought well and bravely under Ali Fuad Bey, and but for this results would have been very different.

I give my criticism below :—

1. It would have been advisable for the Headquarters of the IV Army to keep in close touch with the VIII Army Corps when a serious attack was to be delivered. I cannot in any way approve of its move Northwards.
2. The whole of the enemy operations were directed against Es Salt.

    The enemy wishes to create a strategical bridgehead, whence he can advance later against Amman, Deraa, or Beisan; consequently it is necessary to retake Es Salt at all costs.

    This would be difficult by day as the enemy has so many Machine Guns with his Cavalry, but at night it would always be possible from the North, with Infantry, as the enemy has there only two Cavalry Brigades (1), and later on, indeed, a fifth regiment, besides some artillery.

    Only on the North is co-operation possible with the 3rd Cavalry Division, which has fought splendidly.

    I recommend pushing forward a light screen of Infantry on to the former battle ground at the first sign of the light failing; with this, at dusk, artillery and Machine Guns should come into action.

    The remainder of the Infantry should be collected on the right wing, and should take Es Salt with the bayonet from the North.

    Instead of that, in this morning's report, there appears a statement that the right wing of the Infantry is advancing on Es Salt and that the 8th Cavalry Regiment is already there.
3. I would suggest that in such a position there should not be so much talk of losses and shortage of water. In severe fighting of this kind, losses are inevitable. Water could be brought from Suweileh.

    Other troops have had far greater losses. It is we, as Prussian Officers, who are charged with the duty of pushing forward with the greatest energy, satisfying complaints as far as possible, but otherwise insisting with an iron-like resolution on our wishes.
4. Had the VIII Army Corps taken up the flanking position which I have advised since the beginning of April, such a break through by Cavalry would never have occurred. Water can be no excuse, for there is sufficient in the Jordan, and the men's supplies could have been boiled.
5. I recommend, in the VIII Army Corps' position, to give each cavalry post that has been pushed out, a group of infantry with a Machine gun; these can later be protected by barbed wire. Perhaps this cannot take place everywhere, but it must be done on the most important roads.
6. I have repeatedly drawn attention to the fact that it is necessary to close the important roads at suitable places, or at least prepare them for closing. But on 30th April, at 7.30 a.m. the English were at Jisr Ed Damie with artillery and motors, and shortly before 11 a.m. a few squadrons had arrived opposite El Salt. I am going to send Major Effuert to Es Salt to arrange a few supporting points on decisive heights, the early completion of which I request, if possible with the help of the inhabitants.

    I beg that the above named work may be taken in hand as soon as possible on the roads leading to Es Salt, as well as on the roads leading to Tell Hammam (2). The barricades can be watched during the day by patrols, in order not to employ too many groups. At night they must be manned, also as soon as strong enemy forces are being concentrated West of the Jordan or at the Bridgehead.

7. I recommend alternative positions being prepared for the artillery, and more use made of Dummy positions.

This will lessen our losses.

(Signed) LIMAN VON SANDERS.

(Apparently draft for telegram).

4th May, 1918.

To Major Von Papen,

During the night 3rd Cavalry Division took the heights North of Es Salt, and it is now in immediate possession.

The enemy has retired in a S.W. direction, and is being pursued by a Battalion and some Cavalry moving on a parallel course.

I hold you personally responsible if, through any delay on the part of Shukri Bey's Column, a set back should occur.

I request an immediate report from the scene of fighting.

(Signed) LIMAN VON SANDERS.

N.B.—(1). Liman Von Sanders evidently estimated each Cavalry Brigade at two Regiments.

(2). Close to Ain Hamman, 3 miles S.W. of Amman.

The draft letter below is undated, but from contemporary correspondence is undoubtedly of about 5th May, 1918.

Marshal Liman. Nablus.

Now that the normal situation is restored I respectfully notify your Excellency of the following :—

1. The Army most emphatically protests against the untrue announcement of the 7th Army, that the 3rd Cavalry Division took the heights North of Es Salt.

These heights are covered with the dead of the 66th Infantry Regiment, only one patrol from the 8th Cavalry Regiment was there just as strange is the assertion of the 3rd Cavalry Division, that for two days past they have been in possession of the Western heights, as yesterday evening the English Cavalry entirely unhindered withdrew beyond El Salt in the direction of El Mandesi.

The 66th Infantry Regiment fought very gallantly. Its high losses prove this. If they did not succeed in beating the enemy at the exact moment desired by your Excellency, this was due to circumstances into which I cannot enter in a " Clear " telegram.

However, your Excellency will doubtless agree that when an attack repeatedly ordered does not develop, I should as in duty bound report with regard to the situation as it actually is, and should not make triumphant announcements.

Your Excellency will be satisfied with the bearing of the 8th Army Corps; which during the foregoing weeks has been so equipped and furnished with directions from the Army, that no doubt could prevail as to its task.

2. Your Excellency has complained of deficient reports. In reply to this I respectfully report that the Army Headquarters only had one Telephone Operator at its disposal. The rest of the personnel took part in the defence of Es Salt, and are dead, wounded or prisoners—besides this Headquarters had only one line, generally cut of order, which served at the same time as Operation line. Your Excellency will agree that this line, when in working order should be used first of all for the transmission of Operation Orders. I may add that I had only one Orderly Officer. All other Officers, despite urgent requests were unable to keep up with the Headquarters as they were not mounted.

The Army Headquarters working under such conditions has been for five days continucusly in closest touch with its units. It left ES SALT one minute before the English forced their way in.

It is evident, that the limited communications of the Army Headquarters might give the impression that it was not informed as to the situation during this period. In the same way as a Headquarters established in Nablus, with a great number of good lines. As a matter of fact, the Headquarters were always well informed as to the situation.

3. It must be an error if your Excellency assumes that the Army rushed an unplanned attack against the bridgehead—the Army Headquarters had no such incomprehensible arrangement, but only ordered that the Infantry of the 48th Infantry Division should press forward resolutely into the old positions, and that the Artillery should keep the Jordan Bridges under continuous fire.

4. In yesterday's telegram, your Excellency referred pointedly to my personal responsibility. From this I must assume that your Excellency believes that I was not aware of my responsibility as Chief of Staff, and did not fulfil my duty during these days. This is the first time in my military career that this reproach has been addressed to me.

Therefore I respectfully beg your Excellency to grant my immediate relief from my present position, and to employ me as a Battalion Commander on a battle front.

(Signed) VON PAPEN.

These documents were found in the Yilderin Headquarters, Nazareth.

CAPTURED DOCUMENT.

Letter to KIAZIM PASHA, C.G.S. Yilderin from (apparently the letter is unsigned) DJEMAL PASHA, G.O.C. IV Army.

I humbly thank your Excellency for the kind words which you have been so kind as to addresse to me. In this fifth year of War we are all accustomed to misunderstanding. In the meanwhile the point in question is that the Commander of Army must possess the entire confidence of the Army Group Commander if he is to work successfully.

I learn from the discourse which his Excellency, the Marshal, has directed to me in writing, that the decisions of the Army had not met with the approval of his Excellency.

Your Excellency I beg to be allowed to take the following stand with regard to these criticisms :—

1. The Marshal is of the opinion that Salt should have been taken during the night from the North with the infantry of the 8th Army Corps, while simply a light infantry screen should have left on the front of the 8th Army Corps. This solution which perhaps appears possible according to the map, is as a matter of fact a tactical impossibility.

At the first attack on the morning of 30th April, the foremost positions of the 48th Infantry Division, that is, the right wing of 8th Army Corps, had already been lost.

If the 8th Army Corps was to hold on—which was an absolute necessity then no man could be withdrawn out of its front.

This alone would have been wrong on account of the moral reaction on the troops who were fighting. Till 4 p.m. the Army Command had positive hopes of holding Salt. If the Army Command had withdrawn from here earlier, the defence would have probably have been smashed by midday. The position of the Army Command was therefore close to Salt.

If the Army Command had joined up with the 8th Army Corps after the fall of Es Salt it would have been able to effect this by about 9 p. m.

An order given at this hour for the concentration of the infantry of the 8th Army Corps on its right flank could have been carried out somewhere between 1 and 2 a.m. next morning. An attack on Salt could not have been made with less than 3 Battalions. They would have had to be taken from Lufty Bey's Division which itself is only three Battalions strong. In that case this infantry would have had to carry out a six hours night march from Jebel Hot (unlocated) to Salt from a South Westerly Direction. Hence follows the technical impossibility of the operation required by His Excellency. If it were determined on, the danger was imminent that the front of the VIII Army Corps would be crushed in, and the attack on Salt, which could not be managed with this infantry from the North, would likewise miscarry.

There is not the slightest doubt that Salt must be captured from the enemy again as soon as possible. This could, however, according to views taken here, only come to pass through a co-operation of forces from the direction of Ed Damie and Amman.

The task of the VIII Army Corps was clear. It had to hold on. In consequence of this, the only thing the Army Command could do was to exercise as much influence as possible on the battle front which was developing round Es Salt. Hence the decision to take to the heights to the North of Es Salt, which had already been discussed before, when your Excellency was present.

Had the Army Command joined up with the 8th Corps Commander, then it would have been cut off from every communication and not even in the position to provide for the reinforcements of the VIII Army Corps.

2. The Marshal reproaches the Army for not taking the flank position recommended by him since the beginning of April. If the 48th Division had been situated on a flank position on the Jordan, the rapid break through of the enemy cavalry towards the North would of course have been prevented. I however venture to leave it at the judgement of your Excellency whether the Lufty Division with three Battalions (not yet 1000 strong) would have been in the position to hold the front attack by the 60th Infantry Division; on the other hand I venture to remind your Excellency that the Army has four times requested that the 2nd Caucusus Brigade be placed under it for tactical purposes. This request was rejected. The result was that the 9th Cavalry Regiment immediately withdrew before the enemy cavalry to Mafid Jozele, whilst the 11th Cavalry Regiment obstructed the right flank of the 48th Division; if the 2nd Caucusus Brigade had been attached, it would have been withdrawn into the Mountain passes leading to Salt, and would have delayed the enemy until the weak local defences of Salt could have been strengthened.

3. The Marshal considers that not too much be said in such a position, of losses and scarcity of water. The attack of the 66th Infantry Regiment had come to a complete standstill at noon on the 3rd May, and encountered energetic resistance. The infantry lay on the whole 100 to 200 meters in front of the enemy. Then the telegram from the Marshal arrived that Salt must be taken on that very afternoon. I reported as in duty bound, how things stood and said that it was not possible to continue the attack before night set in—at the same time however, as the action of the enemy seemed to be with regard to the whole position to be threatening, I requested that the pressure on Salt be continued by the 3rd Cavalry Division.

It of course goes without saying that all the difficulties mentioned in the report such as munition supply, and provision of water, have been surmounted, and that we continue the attack with the utmost energy. The Marshal must not therefore construe a faithful report as lack of energy on the part of those beneath him. I have certainly been in a more difficult situation in war than this, but never yet has this reproach been made to me.

Your Excellency will understand that with such differences of opinion, confidential and profitable work is not possible.

An Army Command can demand that tactical decisions which can only be formed on the basis of a judgement made on the spot should not be characterised without further ceremony as entirely unreasonable.

I therefore think it best for all parties if his Excellency the Marshal, responds to the wish I directed to him. I further report briefly to your Excellency on the position here.

It is not improbable that the enemy will shortly make a renewed attempt to capture the East Jordan region.

Considering the importance of an English success in the East Jordan region to the General position of the Army Group, the Army feels bound in duty to make the following proposals :—

A fresh attack may be attempted, with the numerous British Cavalry, by encircling both flanks of the VIII Army Corps (especially the left) with a simultaneous holding down of the front of the Army Corps and the breakthrough of a Cavalry Division East of Jordan towards the North.

The communication in rear of VIII Army Corps must in all circumstances be kept open.

In addition, the following seem necessary to the Army up to the time when it is in itself ready for attack.
(1). A mixed group of all arms for blocking the roads leading to Es Salt with its necessary Mountain Artillery.
(2). Grouping of the 3rd Cavalry Division on the East bank of the Jordan as "action" troops against enemy Cavalry thrusting through towards the North.
(3). Formation of a reinforced Cavalry Brigade (out of the Caucases Cavalry Brigade and 7th Cavalry Regiment) on the left flank of the VIII Army Corps.
(4). Reinforcement of VIII Army Corps in Mountain Artillery.
(5). Better equipment of the Army in Motor Lorry Columns, and mule transport columns, in order to regulate securely the provisioning and munition supply.
(6). Improvement of the Battle leadership and assignment of necessary materials hereto.

All these preparations are considered at the same time as preparations for an offensive against the English Jordan flank.

We are proceeding with the further restorations of those barriers which were already established on the heights of Salt on the occasion of the last attack. Similar barriers are necessary on the heights East of Salt against an enveloping movement from the South.

The Army would be grateful, if Major Effnert could direct this work for some time as the Army Pioneer Inspector has been sick for 8 days.

I beg your Excellency, as far as it seem expedient to you, to give an exposition of my statements as set forth in the foregoing to His Excellency.

(This document was found in the Yilderin Headquarters Nazareth).

APPENDIX "H".

MEMORANDUM BY BRIGADE VETERINARY OFFICER.

The following is the animal wastage of 3rd A.L.H. Brigade covering period from November 1st, 1917, to 31st November 1918.

November and December 1917.

Deaths 163. Evacuations 244.

This covers period of Beersheba—Jerusalem operations and was a exceedingly strenuous time for all animals engaged. The deaths include 115 horses that were either killed in action, killed by bombs or destroyed as a result of wounds. 7 Were destroyed suffering from exhaustion and 6 from laminitis. 8 Died of bowel complaints.

Of those evacuated 100 were evacuated from wounds. The rest were mainly cases of lameness, exhaustion, laminitis and sore backs.

At times during the first forthnight of November, there was a great shortage of water with the resulting loss of vigour amongst the horses. At one stage the whole Brigade, (horses), were without water for from 43 to 58 hours, during which time the work was very strenuous, a lot of it being done at the trot, (after leaving Karm). The longest stretch without water was done by two troops of the 9th Regiment, who went without a drink for 76 hours. At the end of it they looked pretty weary and miserable, and had lost a fair amount of condition, but soon picked up again, after a few days rest.

The average ration for November was 9lbs of grain, (mostly gram), and no hay stuffs. December the grain was the same with the addition of 3 lbs of tibbin and 5 lbs. of hay. The lowest issue was $5\frac{1}{2}$ lbs. of grain for one day, and 6 lbs. for two days, and this when the climatic conditions were very bad.

The most noticeable change took place in the horses after the cold rainy weather came on, and then they lost condition rapidly and a number had to be avacuated for debility.

Considering the conditions sore backs were remarkably few, and it was over a fortnight after leaving Shellal before any had to be evacuated for that reason, and then only 3. Later on, of course, there were more.

January and February 1918

Deaths 14. *Evacuations* 103.

Included amongst the evacuations are a number of debility cases as the result of the previous operations.

Tibbin was only issued for a few veterinary cases during these months.

March and April 1918.

Deaths 17. *Evacuations.* 109.

36 of those evacuated were suffering from debility and the rest were mainly injuries, and cases of lameness.

May 1918.

Deaths 23. *Evacuations* 55.

This period covers the Es Salt operations, where there 10 horses killed and 24 wounded.

June and July 1918.

Deaths 66. *Evacuations* 208.

43 of the deaths were from a bomb raid. 71 Animals were also wounded in the same raid, 6 of which were afterwards destroyed in Mobile Veterinary Section.

Amongst the evacuations were 39 wounded horses and 58 cases of skin disease, most of which were probably mange.

August and Sept. 1918.

Deaths 30. *Evacuations* 161.

18 of the deaths were horses killed in action in the Damascus operations.

October and November 1918.

Deaths 103. *Evacuations* 136.

There was very little wastage during the end of September, so that the above, (October and November), period practically covers the wastage during the operations through Damascus, Homs and back to Tripoli. The horses stood the trip to Damascus exceptionally well. The day the Brigade went though the town, the work was fairly strenuous and a few of them dropped out, but this was mainly due to shortage of fodder, most of the horses not having had a feed since the previous afternoon.

Sore backs were very prevalent after reaching Damascus. In my opinion they were due mainly to the rifle buckets which had only been issued to the Units a little over a week before the Brigade left Ludd. I took a census of the sore backs and found that 62 % of the sores were on the rifle bucket side, (off side), and the remaining 38 % anywhere else on the back.

The last 24 hours of the trek to Homs was very hard on the horses, owing to the shortage of water, none of which was available for them for the last 45 miles, with the result that several became exhausted and had to be destroyed.

During November the D. V. S. ordered the destruction of any sick horses over 12 years of age, and also any under that age that would take over two months treatment to cure them. This accounts for the large number of deaths during this period.

Units on mobilisation were issued with rather a variety of horses, it being quite evident that each buyer had his own opinion as to the class of animal most suitable for active service. There is a very old saying that "horses will gallop all shapes" and in a way this applies to horses on active service, when they have to undergo privations of all sorts and still carry a man and equipment, as there are horses of all shapes and sizes that have been right through everything and done their work well right through. In my opinion there is one class of horse, (if it may be called a class), that has stood out above the others as far as hard work and keeping condition is concerned and that is a low thick set animal, 14.3 to 15.2 in height, short backed, well ribbed up and showing a bit of breeding, age about 7 years to 12 years.

The finer bred horses did their work well, but when it came to hardships they could not keep their condition like the above mentioned and were consequently more liable to sore backs.

The big coarse horse held condition fairly well but wasn't up to the fast work.

(Sgd). S. A. MOUNTJOY, *Major*,
B. V. O., 3rd L. H. Bde.

APPENDIX "J".

Decorations awarded to members of Brigade since 27/10/17

Headquarters.
D.S.O. Brigadier-General L. C. Wilson, C.M.G.
        Major W. M. Anderson.
M.C.   Captain W. M. Lyall.

8th Light Horse Regiment.
D.S.O. Major H. J. Shannon   Major L. A. W. Mac Pherson, M.C.
M.C.   Lieut. L. A. W. Mac Pherson Lieut. T. R. Peppercorn.
        Captain W. McGrath.   Lieut. R. H. Borbridge.
        Lieut. J. N. Stubbs.
D.C.M. 340, Sergt. W.N.J. Bowman   1010, Sergt. H. W. Keable.
        353, S.S.M. A. H. Currington 954, Sergt. J. E. Chapman.
        889, S.S.M. K. C. Lawler.   648, Corpl. W. W. Willis.
M.M.   Nos. 405, T/Cpl. S. J. Kerr. 1176, Tpr. E. S. Ackland.
        3193, Tpr. L. Taylor.   1418, Sergt. L. Julian.
        3237, Tpr. J. J. Gallagher. 3466, Sergt. E. M. Williams.
        1666, L/Cpl. J. Thompson.   3507, Tpr. H. A. Schier.
        2952, L/Cpl. A. E. Perry.

Chev. of Crown of Roumania.   Lieut. R. H. Borbidge, M.C.

Medaille Militaire.   1300, L/Cpl. W. C. Sherwill.

9th Light Horse Regiment.
C.M.G.
        Lieut.-Col. W. H. Scott, D.S.O.
D.S.O. Major T. J. Daly.   Major H. M. Parsons.
Bar to D.S.O.
        Lieut.-Col. W. H. Scott, C.M.G., D.S.O.
M.C.   Captain E. M. Luxmore.   Lieut. J. N. McDonald.
        Lieut. R. C. Sharp.   Lieut. L. M. S. Hargrave.
        Lieut. N. F. Wastell.
D.C.M. S/Sergt. H. J. Cattle.   Cpl. G. F. Cruddas.
        902 Signr. J. N. Smythe.   1458 Sig. N. C. Halliday
        255 Sergt. J. L. Foreman.   769, T/Cpl. A. H. Todd.
        956 Cpl. H. E. Runn.
M.M.   1004, Tpr. W. H. Watson.   821, T/Cpl. H. D. Hillgrove.
        2809, L/Cpl. R. L. W. Dennison. 605A, Tpr. F. R. Morgan.
        608A, T/Sergt. J. R. Forrester. 580, Sergt. H. C. Maxwell.
        2830, Tpr. W. P. Whittlesea. 1212, Tpr. E. K. Smith.
696,   Tpr. J. Carroll.   213A, Tpr. N. L. Partington.
271,   Tpr. T. W. Harvey.   504, T/S.S.M. B. G. Wuchatsch.
1442,   Cpl. C. Rodger.

10th L. H. Regt.
C.M.G. Lieut.-Col. T. J. Todd, D.S.O.
D.S.O. Major A. C. N. Olden.   Major H. B. Hamlin.
Bar to D.S.O.   C.M.G. Lieut.-Col. T. J. Todd, D.S.O.

M.C.	Lieut. F. J. McGregor.	2/Lt. A. W. M. Thompson.
	2/Lt. C. Foulkes-Taylor.	Lieut. E. F. Richardson.
	2/Lt. P. W. K. Doig.	Capt. G. Rosevear.
D.C.M.	129, Sergt. C. B. Rickards.	137, Sergt. F. C. P. Salmond.
	245, Sergt. G. J. Connolly.	2426, Tpr. R. J. Louden.
	1340, T/Sergt. W. C. Martin.	30, Sergt J. Fitzmaurice.
	1178, T/Cpl. W. J. Langdon.	
M.M.	3427, Tpr. W. I. Mewton.	975, Tpr. A. E. Wallace.
	1116, Tpr. A. B. Bremner,	400, T/Sgt. D. H. Finlay.
	1314, L/Cpl. B. M. Craig	1438, Tpr. T. H. Sarre.
	726, Tpr. Z. Green.	1382, Tpr. J. Edwards.
	236, L/Cpl. E. G. Beard.	359, T/Cpl. J. McKenna.
	1170, T/Cpl. C. P. E. Fraser.	1434 Tpr. J. W. Spillman.
	1022, Sergt. J. V. Hay.	
O.B.E.	Hon. Major P. P. Buckland.	

3rd. Machine Gun Squadron.

M.C.	Lieut. R. R. W. Patterson M. M.	
D.C.M.	1412, Sergt. A. F. McLeod.	58, Sergt. H. E. Saunders.
	1621, Cpl. S. E. Broard.	237, Cpl. C. W. Beswick.
	214, Cpl. N. J. Nyde.	
M.M.	323 L/Cpl. E. R. McGiunness.	2447 L/Cpl. J. Antonio.
	1336, L/Cpl. W. F. Liddelow.	2398, L/Cpl. A. J. Randall.

3rd. Signal Troop.

D.C.M.	588, Corpl. J. Fraser.
M.M.	590, 2/Cpl. A. S. Goldthrope.
	1376, Sapper W. H. Bruce.

THE THIRD LIGHT HORSE BRIGADE
AUSTRALIAN IMPERIAL FORCE

in

THE EGYPTIAN REBELLION 1919

---oOo---

NARRATIVE

of

Brig.General L.C.Wilson, C.B., C.M.G., D.S.O., V.D., G.O.C. 3rd L.H. Bde. A.I.F.

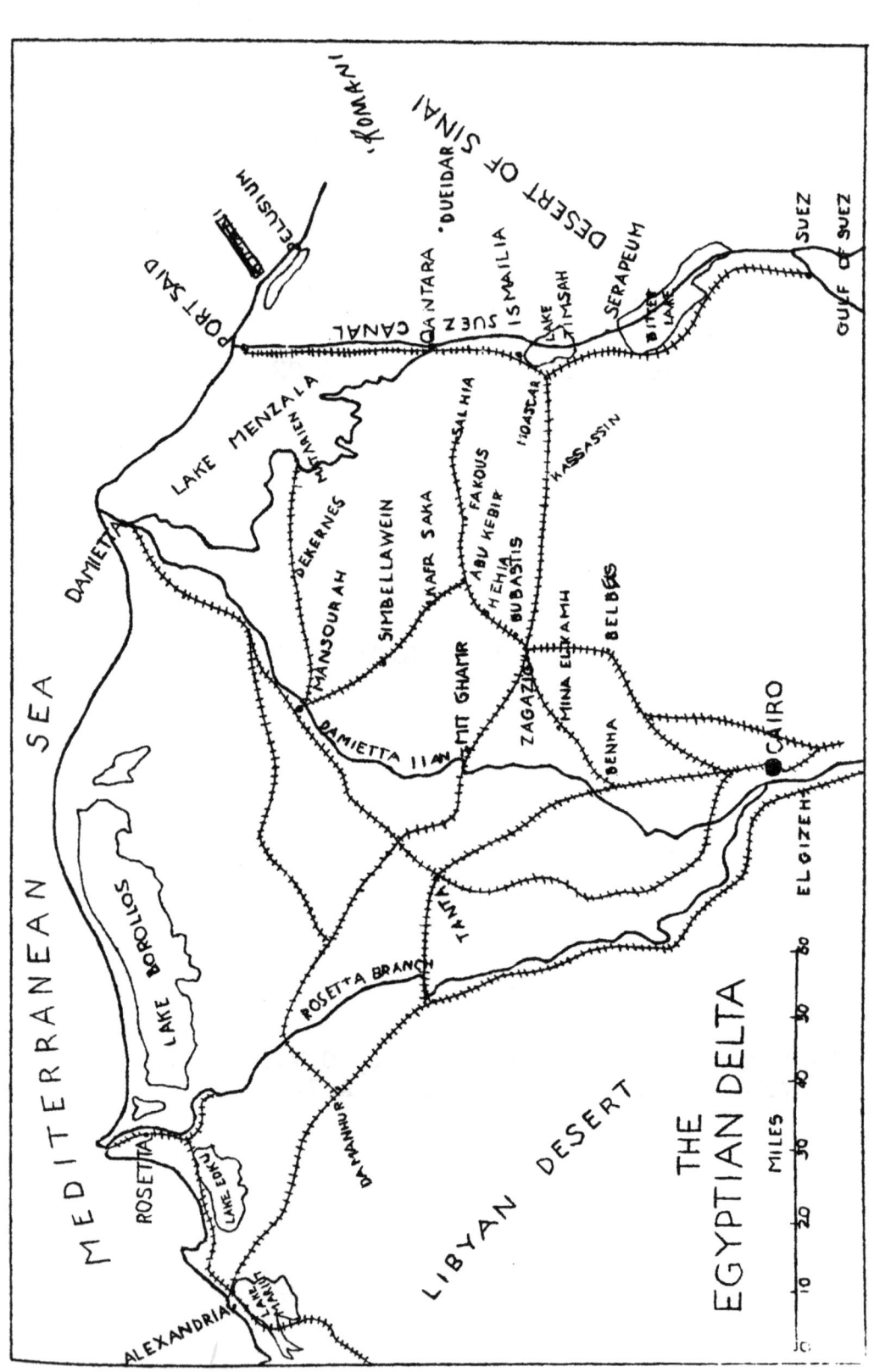

THE THIRD LIGHT HORSE BRIGADE
AUSTRALIAN IMPERIAL FORCE
in
THE EGYPTIAN REBELLION OF 1919

---oOo---

Narrative by Brig.-Gen. L. C. Wilson, C.B., C.M.G., D.S.O., V.D., G.O.C. 3rd L.H. Bde. A.I.F.

PART 1

Up to the moment when War broke out with Turkey in November 1914, Egypt was still nominally a Province of the Turkish Empire. Its foreign and internal position was stabilised by a British Army of occupation. The internal administration of the Country was carried on by a Council of Ministers in the name of The Khedive. The Council of Ministers was assisted by British advisers who really controlled the administration of the Country. When War broke out the Khedive, who was at that time in Constantinople, adhered to the enemy. He was accordingly deposed, and a Sultan independent of Turkey was appointed, and Egypt was declared to be a British Protectorate. The Country placidly accepted the position during the War. The enemy's scheme in 1915 and 1916 was to raise a rebellion in Egypt, which was to facilitate the Turkish invasion from the East and the Senussi attack from the West. In this it was hoped that all the Bedouins in Western Egypt and particularly the Fayum region would join. This scheme came to nothing. After the Armistice Pasha Zaghlul formed a new Nationalist Party, but no doubt a great deal of preparatory and organising work had been done during the period of War.

Zaghlul thought to give his programme the appearance of strict legality, basing his demands, mainly, on the avowed War aims of the Allies and the doctrine of President Wilson with regard to self determination.

In this way he managed to secure the adherence of many of the Moslems and, remarkably enough, of the Copts, who, as a body, are naturally moderate in politics and had hitherto been opposed to all Moslem nationalist schemes.

The attitude of the Copts was of interest, and incidentally a great compliment to British forbearance. Canon David J. Garland, a Chaplain attached to the Australian Forces, tells me that following a suggestion made by the Military Authorities, he interviewed certain of the Copts, Ecclesiastical and Lay, to ascertain their reason for their unprecedented alliance with the Moslems. The Copts quite ingenuously told him that they were frightened to go against the Egyptians, because if the Egyptians won they would renew their persecution of the Copts. On the other hand, if the British won they were so good that they would not punish the Copts for rebelling. The Canon felt that it would be useless to make any appeal to them as it might do more harm than good, by giving the impression that we could not win without their help. By making the retention of the Capitulations a plank in his Platform, Zaghlul also appealed to the sympathies of certain of the non-British European residents of Egypt, particularly the French and the Italians.

Zaghlul's great point was that he had waited until the Allies had won the War and signed the Armistice. From that moment he claimed that the Protectorate, which was accepted as a War measure, had ceased to have any legal justification, and declared that the Protectorate had lapsed, and that the Egyptians were not bound to recognise any laws of the British or of the British controlled Egyptian Government. He demanded the right to send delegates to the Peace Conference which was then sitting in Paris. This claim was refused by the British Government. Zaghlul's supporters became very truculent and finally three of the principals were arrested and deported. This was the signal for the launching of the movement organised by Zaghlul. Disorders immediately broke out in the cities, and then spread to the provinces.

Some explanation is necessary as to why the Nationalist movement spread so thoroughly in the country districts. As in India, the British Government for some years past had adopted a Policy of Public Education. The result of this was that a large number of young Egyptians were highly educated in the public schools and educational establishments of Egypt, who, when they arrived at manhood, found that they were unable to obtain positions in which their educational abilities could be regularly employed. They looked around and found that all the higher positions in the Government of the Country were in the hands of British Officers, and naturally asked why they, native Egyptians, should not fill these positions. Although we would not agree with them, they considered themselves quite qualified so to do, and there thus grew up a very large and influential "effendi" class who wanted the British as the governing body withdrawn from Egypt. There were some other difficulties, the result of the War, which created an ill-feeling against the British administration, and these were the questions of labour supplied to the Army and the requisitioning of grain and crops during the War.

During the War a very large number of Egyptians were used on the Palestine back-war areas as labour battalions amounting, at times, to considerably over 100,000 men. These men were recruited in Egypt for short periods of, say three months each, the system being to requisition each village for so many men. Under the system existing in Egypt all requisitions to a village go through the Omdah, or Mayor, of that village, and he makes the necessary arrangements for the supply of the labour or articles requisitioned. This system gave the Omdah very great power. In the first place, he had the selection of the labourers who were to go. Working in a labour battalion in the war zone was not looked forward to by the Egyptian villagers with any great pleasure, particularly as a large number of them failed to come back through disease or privation. The Omdah was able to pick on to those persons in a village whom he did not like or who would not pay him for exemption, and all complaints made by those selected were answered by the Omdah that he was acting under direct instructions of the British Officials. The result of this was that there was great resentment against the British Government because of this forced labour.

Another cause of great dissatisfaction in Egypt was the requisitioning of grain. In accordance with the system a requisition was issued to the Omdah, who undertook the duty of collecting the grain from the various farmers. There might, for the sake of example, be fifty farmers on whom he would make requisitions for a certain proportion of their grain. This grain was duly supplied and was supposed to be paid for. The British Government certainly paid for it, but paid the money to the Omdah. The Omdah then distributed as much, or as little, of this money as he thought advisable amongst the farmers. A large number of these farmers he omitted to pay, and when they complained afterwards that they had not received payment, he blamed the British Government for failure to pay. The result was that a very large number

of farmers throughout Egypt during the War supplied grain for
which they received no payment, and the only satisfaction they
got was that they were told the British Government had failed
to pay for it.   This alleged failure to pay for grain, and
the injustices consequent on the labour supply system, created
an ill-feeling amongst the country people which had never
existed before against the British Government.

     The first active disorders began in Egypt in the month
of March 1919.   It was rather unfortunate for the Egyptians
that they started at that time.   It would have been much
better for them if the rebellion had been postponed for about
another month.   Immediately after the Armistice with Germany
in November 1918, arrangements were made for the repatriation
of the bulk of the troops in the Eastern war area, and by
March 1919 practically the whole of the British Troops and
Indian Troops, with the exception of the permanent garrisons
for Palestine and the Prisoners of War camps in Egypt, had
returned to England or to India.

     The two Australasian Mounted Divisions still remained
in Egypt, but at the beginning of March they had commenced to
demobilise.   By the middle of March the first Light Horse
Brigade had left for Home, and arrangements were in hand to
send the rest of the four Australian Brigades still in Egypt
to their Homeland.   The remainder of the Anzac Mounted Division was at Rafa and the Australian Mounted Division was at
Moascar on the Canal.   A few more weeks would have seen
these mounted troops out of Egypt and there would have remained in Egypt only a few details and a couple of Indian Infantry
Battalions on garrison duty at the Prisoners of War Camp.
When the disturbances commenced there were four complete Australian Mounted Brigades and part of the New Zealand Mounted
Brigade in Egypt, available for service.

     The insurrection at once took the form of a destruction
of all means of communications.   Telephone and telegraph
wires were cut and railway lines destroyed.   Most of the
railways in the agricultural districts were laid on sleepers
along sides of Canals.   The procedure of the insurgents was
to remove the fish plates at the end of a section of, say, 50
yards of railway line, then several hundred men lifted the
rails and sleepers bodily and threw the lot into the adjoining Canal.   Christian Churches throughout the country were
marked down for destruction and were promptly destroyed.
Christians in the country towns were attacked and murdered,
particularly Armenians, British Officers and tourists proceed-

ing to upper Egypt on holidays were attacked in the train and several of them were murdered and so mutilated with sticks that their bodies could not be identified.

Shortly after the commencement of the trouble General Allenby was appointed High Commissioner for Egypt, and as such had dictatorial power. A general movement was in evidence among the natives to embarrass the administration and paralyse the general routine of life in Egypt. Strikes on a large scale were planned to take place and a general strike was called involving Government Offices and State Services, such as the Army, the Police and the Railways, and there were reports that there would be an outbreak of incendiarism in the English quarters. A strike was arranged of lawyers and students, although I do not believe that it would have done the British Administration any great harm if the Native lawyers and students had gone out on strike.

Towards the end of March a change came over public opinion in Egypt and the general strike did not eventuate. The moderates and the foreign residents recognised that public security was collapsing, and if they wanted safety they would have to ask for support and help from the British Military Forces. In some of the villages in the Delta, Soviet Governments were formed for Local Administration and for local safety.

Of the fifteen mounted regiments of the A.I.F. fourteen had operated in the Eastern Theatre. Four of these - the 1st, 2nd, 3rd and 4th, had left for Australia prior to the breaking out of the rebellion. Of the ten remaining regiments seven, namely, 7th, 8th, 9th, 10th, 11th, 14th and 15th, were operating with Headquarters at Zagazig under my command and of the remaining three, the 5th and 6th were at Damanhaur near Alexandria, and the 12th was on the Nile above Cairo. These three last mentioned regiments were engaged in work similar to that being done by the 3rd Brigade and its attached four regiments, but this narrative is confined to the operations of the troops controlled by me. At times two of my own regiments, the 8th and 9th, were detached for duty in the Bilbeis Sector. None of the other Australian Brigadier-Generals were available, as Cox of the 1st had gone to Australia, Ryrie of the 2nd had taken charge of A.I.F. Administrative Headquarters at Moascar, Grant of the 4th and Macarthur Onslow of the 5th were both ill. Upon taking over command at Zagazig, Judge J. J. Kershaw of the Supreme Court, and Mr. James F. Hopkins of the Finance Department of the Egyptian Government, were attached to my headquarters. These gentlemen were of great service to us, as they could and did advise on many matters where a knowledge of native character and psychology was of the utmost importance.

PART II

The Third Light Horse Brigade (8th, 9th and 10th Regiments) had arrived at Moascar from Syria on the 6th March, 1919, and during the next week preliminary arrangements were being made for demobilization, horses, transport and part of equipment being handed in. Prior to the 13th March we took little interest in local Egyptian affairs, but on that date the first rumour of trouble came to us when orders were received for the detailing of an inlying piquet of 20 men under an officer for use in case of possible civil disturbances in Ismalia. This was the first step in operations which kept the Australians and New Zealanders under active service conditions until our final departure in July 1919.

On the 15th orders were received from Division to send two parties of 3 officers and 50 other Ranks each to Zagazig and Minet el Qamh respectively to guard the Railway Stations at those places. Both these towns lie on the Ismalia-Cairo Railway. Zagazig is a town of some 40,000 inhabitants and Minet el Qamh is smaller. One party was detailed from the 8th Regiment under Major Macpherson and the other from the 10th Regiment under Capt. Palmer. Both parties were on the train within an hour from receipt of orders.

On the 16th March a small disturbance took place at Ismalia, but this was soon put down by the picquets. On the same day a party of 15 was sent to Quassasin to guard the Canal lock there. Quassasin was the scene of the midnight cavalry charge in 1881 when the British Cavalry made their famous attack.

Captain Palmer's party from the 10th Regiment, consisting of 3 officers and 50 O.R., arrived by train at Minet el Qamh and posted various picquets, including one at the Railway Station. The local rioters here made no secret of what they intended to do to the new arrivals and the old adage of "forewarned is forearmed" again proved its truth. About 10.45 next morning a mob of about 1,000 rioters made a rush at a post commanded by Lt. Macgregor and twenty men. This mob was armed with stones and sticks, and stoned the post.

After being ordered to halt they got within 10 yards of the post when the Officer in charge gave the order to fire. The mob at once broke and the order to cease fire was given. One of our aeroplanes fired two short bursts into the rioters. During the few seconds that firing continued 39 natives were killed and 25 wounded. When the mob broke a large number of them tried to escape by swimming across the adjoining canal - "the river of Moses" and in so doing some 40 of them were drowned. The post had one casualty - a trooper was wounded in the neck by a bullet. The lesson had been severe, but there was no more rioting at Minet el Qamh.

On the 16th March orders were issued for the patrolling of the Railway Line between Ismalia and Zagazig by 3 mounted Squadrons and for one Squadron of the 8th Regiment to proceed to Zagazig by route march.

Orders were issued that before machine or Lewis gun fire was employed against rioters, every eleventh round should be withdrawn from belts and drums. This was to break the automatic firing at every tenth shot and so compel the gunner to deliberately start again if the occasion required it.

On the 17th March Orders were received for all fighting troops of the Brigade to proceed to Zagazig. The first party moved off under the command of Lt. Col. Scott of the 9th Regiment. A large part of the Brigade equipment had been handed in and great energy was displayed in recovering it or fresh equipment. Some was obtained from Kantara. The following morning, the 18th March, the remainder of the Brigade entrained but was held up at Kassassin owing to the line having been destroyed at that place. The break having been repaired, the train arrived at Zagazig on the morning of the 19th. Brigade Headquarters were established at the Irrigation Office, and the Brigade came under the orders of G.O.C. No.1 Sector, whose headquarters were at Benha. The necessary defensive arrangements were at once made. The policy at present was to confine our attention to the main railway line in order to keep open communication between Cairo and Port Said. With this in view various posts were placed on the Railway and arrangements made for patrols along such line.

On the 19th March a Post of 1 N.C.O. and 3 men on railway guard four miles from Zagazig was rushed by a large party of natives. The natives pretended to be a wedding party and were allowed to get within a few yards of the Post, which they then rushed and disarmed. Three of the four men were roughly handled, the Corporal subsequently dying of his injuries. Two of the men got to a railway cabin from whence they telephoned for assistance. This was promptly forthcoming in the form of a mounted troop and the three injured men were transferred to Hospital.

On the 20th March a conflict took place with some natives on the Zagazig-Belbeis Line, where a post of 1 N.C.O. and 12 O.R. had been placed. Three men from the Post, two of whom were armed, went into a neighbouring village at the invitation of a villager to get some firewood. While in the doorway of the yard where the wood was stored the party was rushed, the two with rifles being pushed inside. One man was knocked down with a piece of wood and his rifle seized, while the second was attacked by some five natives who tried to take his rifle. Meanwhile the third man outside had alarmed the Post, five of whom burst open the door of the yard where they found one of their comrades unconscious and the other struggling with five or six natives. The natives then attacked the rescuers. Fire was opened on the natives, four of whom were killed and one wounded.

Report having been received of the likelihood of an extension of civil disturbances, orders were sent out for all troops to be in a state of preparedness. Machine guns were mounted on Brigade H.Q. and a post of one officer and 20 O.R. with machine guns took possession of the Roof (flat) of the Nudireh (Town Hall). A detachment of 3 officers and 75 O.R. was sent to Belbeis to come under the orders of the Post Commandant there. At this place were the headquarters of the Remounts, and it was arranged that the detachment should be mounted there. Arrangements were made for patrolling Zagazig throughout the night and for dispersing hostile meetings. No drastic action had to be taken in Zagazig against the natives as the show of force was quite sufficient to keep them quiet. Their energies ran to putting up Turkish flags, which, however, they promptly pulled down when ordered to do so.

On the 21st March a Mounted Patrol under Lt. Burns moved at 5.15 a.m. from Zagazig to Mit Gamr, a large town some 20 miles to the north-west, passing through numerous villages en route. The villagers appeared restless but as usual they were ignored, and the patrol arrived at Mit Gamr at noon. They found a British Officer and 15 O.R. (B. 3 class men) engaged on Railway work. The mob had wrecked some of the railway, destroyed some of the carriages and cut all telephone and telegraph lines. They were very hostile to the British party and to some Greek residents. It was decided that these people should all come back to Zagazig with the Patrol. Many breaks in the railway line were observed. The Omdah of the village nearest to each break was ordered to get out a working party to pull the rails and sleepers out of the Canal. This order they promptly observed under the veiled threat that something very unpleasant would happen if they did not.

  This morning in Zagazig a mob of several thousand were demonstrating in the streets. I sent a patrol of 40 mounted men and 120 dismounted into the town. The demonstrators were soon dispersed. One of the rioters raised a rifle against the mounted patrol, one of whom promptly charged him with his sword and put him out of action. It was not safe for men to go about the streets singly, while on the other hand, four of our men on their guard were more than a match for any number of natives. We were fortunate as regards arms, having rifles, bombs, automatic rifles and machine guns. The trouble with our men was to get them to take the natives seriously. In most cases where we had men hurt, it was through not taking any precautions. The natives had been distributing propaganda in bad English amongst our troops in which they called upon their brother Australians to join with them in obtaining freedom. The men laughed at these effusions as even our most rabid Socialists refused to admit brotherhood with the native Egyptians.

  On the 22nd March a railway construction train was sent out by the local Railway Officials to Mit Ghamr to repair the line to that town. I had not been asked to make provision for its protection, nor was I advised that the train was proceeding on the unguarded lines. Late in the afternoon I was informed that the train was stuck up at Kilo 23 as the rails had been torn up on the Zagazig side of the train. At 7.30 p.m. an engine with trucks preceded by a railway trolley as pilot moved out with an escort under Lt. Hay and 25 O.R. The escort's instructions were to bring back the first train, if practicable, but in any case to provide for its safety. A construction train would go out in the morning to help in the reinstatement of the line. Lt. Hay duly arrived at Kilo 23 where the break was. He left his train with an escort and marched into Mit Ghamr, where he found the first train with its crew and guard safe.

A self-appointed Vigilance Committee had taken over the government of the City and relations between the natives and the British party were very strained. At 1.30 p.m. the local inhabitants appeared very hostile, so Lt. Hay and party moved back to Kilo 23. There they found Lt. Lunn and his mounted patrol. This patrol had left Zagazig at dawn, as I had not heard anything of the two trains that had left the previous day. The mounted patrol on the way out had come in contact with a party of 2,000 natives engaged in breaking up the Railway Line. The natives showed fight and carried Turkish flags. The patrol opened fire and killed 30, the rest at once dispersed.

Following Lunn's mounted patrol from Zagazig a railway trolley, with a Vickers-Maxim was sent along the line, and was manhandled across the breaks. After Lt. Lunn passed the rioters again proceeded to break up the line and the trolley came in touch with a crowd of 2,000 to 3,000 natives engaged in burning the Railway Station at Kilo 18. The trolley patrol ran three belts through its machine gun and dispersed the mob, after inflicting some 50 casualties.

The construction train, with an escort under Lt. Middleditch and 20 O.R. and a picquet under Capt. Archer and 60 O.R. of the 14th L.H. Regiment, moved out from Zagazig. Small posts were dropped at intervals to prevent the line being interfered with after the train had passed. The railway trolley above mentioned acted as pilot to the construction train. The construction train joined up with the other two trains and Lt. Lunn's patrol at Kilo 23. The whole party then turned back towards Zagazig. A large mob of natives got on the line with the apparent intention of cutting off the three trains from Zagazig. A Lewis gun on the first train opened fire on them, killing 10, and the mob dispersed. The three trains were then formed into one and with the trolley as pilot returned to Zagazig, picking up the posts that had been dropped in the morning. We had no further trouble on this branch line, and although no posts were left along it, the line was in no way subsequently interfered with.

On 22nd March a motor lorry patrol under Lt. Richardson and 25 O.R. of the 10th Regiment proceeded along the railway line towards Hehia. They found numerous breaks in the line and at two places found natives engaged in the work of destruction. On these occasions they opened fire and dispersed the offenders. Numerous bridges and all telephone and telegraph lines had been destroyed, and in places ditches had been cut across the road.

On the 23rd March Lt. Kildea with 32 O.R. of the 9th Regiment left Zagazig at 6.30 a.m. for Faqus on the Salhia line, 20 miles to the north-east of Zagazig. He found the railway line broken in numerous places and the Christian Churches and several business places at Faqus looted. He camped there for the night and returned to H.Q. at 4 p.m., bringing with him some 20 Europeans (Greeks) who were afraid to remain in the villages.

Starting the same day Lt. Streeter with a troop of the 8th Regiment proceeded through the villages to Saqkr on the Mansura Line, a distance of 20 miles from Zagazig. He found the railway line, telegraph and telephone lines destroyed in numerous places, sleepers and poles being removed to the villages. On two occasions he found natives engaged in destroying the railway line. These he fired upon and dispersed, inflicting a few casualties. He camped at Saqkr for the night and returned next day to Zagazig, bringing with him a few Greek refugees.

On the 25th March an armoured train with a construction gang and 3 Officers and 100 O.R. of the 10th Regiment under Major Hamlin moved out from Zagazig for Mit Ghamr with instructions to restore the line to that place and take rations for the New Zealand Mounted Rifles who were passing through the neighbourhood. The train was preceded by a motor trolley armed with a Vickers-Maxim and a Hotchkiss Automatic. The line had been badly pulled about and there were scores of breaks in it. A similar method to that adopted on the Mansura Line was applied. The local villagers were escorted down to the break and pushed into the Canal and made to pull the sleepers and rails out and put them back in their original places. On one occasion the villagers resisted and one was shot, and two, who attempted to break guard, were bayonetted. The Line was restored for traffic and the party returned to Zagazig the following afternoon. The Line was not again interfered with by the natives.

The villagers had been deceived as to the true position of affairs. They had been told that the Irish would not fire on them, that the Australians were fighting the English in Cairo, that at least 50 Australians were murdered every night in Zagazig and that there would soon be none of them left, and unfortunately for the villagers they believed it too.

The Native Governor of the Province invited me, the G.O.C., to an official dinner. I and three of my senior officers attended, also four of the Senior British Administrators. It was a great success as a dinner, but the humour of it was that with the knowledge of how Mahomet Ali had treated his guests, the chiefs of the Mamelukes, on a similar occasion, we all had loaded revolvers in our tunic pockets and a strong guard was detailed to wait around the corner and join in as soon as a row started. Fortunately, the dinner went off without the revolvers doing likewise.

As means for promptly quelling disturbances we had an armoured Rolls Royce with machine guns and six motor lorries. We commandeered all the motor cars and motor cycles that we saw. The owners were, of course, subsequently compensated for any loss they sustained in this respect.

I was authorised to convene Military Courts to deal with natives for offences against public order, with power to sentence from flogging up to death.

The following is a specimen of local propaganda:-

"BE NOT THE OTHER SLAVE WHEN GOD MADE YOU FREE.- SONS OF THE NILE.

Rather death than shame. Rather die than lie. Rather a sword stroke defending honour, and exalting above meanness, than death in bed. It is more preferable for a man descending from Heaven to be abducted by birds, rather than swallowing cups of scorn, and being watered with which exceeds injury. Calamity extended patience exhausted. The knife reached the bones, we reached to a condition which a noble cannot bear. Bleeding hearts. Shedding tears. Turned cheeks. Restrained souls. Binding tongues. Fettered hands. Robbed Provinces polluted fame. Defamed honour. Vanished dignity, whose leaves withered. Severe injustice erected its ropes, surrounding peaceful villages. Pickaxes of destruction came over. The not educated people invalidated the lasses who are like concealed precious stones, and their hearts are deprived from kindness. The ground is dyed with the blood of the guiltless souls, but of crying from injustice, devils and savage people whose policy is unbearable. These are some of the inflictions you abide under, fearing them, they subdued you, by your silence they aimed the thunderbolts of sufferings against you, rained you a heavy shower of grief, compelled you to sink into the earth and vanish.

What befell upon you, that your flames extinguished your zeal and subsided, you became cowed, you stood with fettered hands answering no call, unable to protect your women, could not preserve honour, could not save blood, and never demanded for your Holy Right.

Did you acquire your objects, have your souls revived, that you escaped from bondage and broke the fetters seizing your necks, and the bonds tieing you, and the robes strapping your arms, or have theequivocal enemy's words enticed you, whose hearts quaked when they feared your power. His promises to you are like a mirage of a pool, the thirsty thinks it water, when he comes near finds it nothing. Has your heroism dissolved? Did brightness of swords, neighing of horses, the crowd of army, rustling of gunsblow up your hearts? You know when the intentions of the resolution of a nation unite, flee the solidity of iron, demolish the mountains, melt the blades in scabbards, and when their hands come together, form a large squadron, whose swords never break, and no demand is difficult to them.

Ye sons of Egypt, awake from your sleep, avoid every dispute and discouragement, never fear encounter, caution saves not from fate. Escaping grants no delay for the appointed time.

Patience is a reason of victory. Rather piercing a throat than back. Prepare for them what you can, fight them with all what you can, Strike over the necks, split the heads, bury them in tombs alive, throw them with burned arrows, whose flames the water cannot extinguish. Give them to drink extreme hot water to cut their intestines and roast their livers; and be sure you will overcome them, and after awhile, they will regret, will go out of it with lowliness. Demanding of truth never loses help and victory from God. Never fear while you are victorious. God is with you, guides you, tranquilizes your thoughts, if you are with Him, will make you victorious and your feet steady."

"A Party of the Free Egyptians"

On the 25th March a patrol of 3 officers and 60 O.R. of the 9th Regiment under Capt. Luxmore, was sent to Simbellawein, 35 miles to the north of Zagazig on the railway line to Mansourah, followed up with an engine and truck with spare fish plates and bolts. They found the railway line broken in numerous places and sleepers and telegraph poles removed and some of the bridges destroyed. On one occasion a native fired on the patrol with the result that the native was shot. Where sleepers had been removed or thrown into the Canal, the local Omdah was given so many hours' notice in which to have them restored. The invitation was in most cases accepted. Where acquiescence was not prompt the adjoining villages were surrounded and all able-bodied men were shepherded down to the Canal into which the rails, with sleepers attached, had been thrown. The natives were then pushed into the Canal and ordered to bring out the rails and sleepers and put them back on the rail-bed from which they had been removed. This they did, and the breakdown gang in the railway truck bolted the rails together again and so restored the line.

Amongst the natives were several of the "Effendi" class, the gentlemen who were responsible for the disturbances. They, in their black coats and patent leather boots, were very supercilious until the Troop Leader had them pushed into the Canal to give their countrymen a hand in getting out the rails. The villagers, with a sense of humour, thought this a great joke. The patrol returned to H.Q. on the 27th.

On 27th March a patrol of the 14th L.H. Regiment, under Major Nobbs, moved out from Zagazig and returned to Abu Kebir on the 31st, passing through Faqus and Salhia. All villages within 1½ miles of the Line were visited and the Omdahs and Sheiks interviewed. Where Canals lay across the line of march the saddles were taken across in boats and the horses swam across. Where breaks occurred in the railway line the Omdahs of the adjoining villages were ordered to restore same forthwith. Several native agitators were arrested and sent into H.Q. The inhabitants were quiet and created no disturbance. It was reported to the C.O. that a party of 15 natives with arms were at an adjoining village, but upon a patrol being sent to the village the armed natives made off without displaying any desire to make contact with our men.

On the 29th March a party was sent to restore the railway between Zagazig and Salhia, and between Zagazig and

Mansourah. The party was placed under the command of Lt. Martin of the 10th Regiment, who, in civil life, was an engineer and railway contractor. These Lines had been destroyed in numerous places. All the line was completely restored by the evening of the 2nd April, with the exception of one bridge. Similar methods to those previously adopted were used for obtaining the natives' co-operation.

As an example of a fine report, that of Lt. Martin is set out in full in the appendix hereto.

The Brigade area, thenceforth called the Zagazig Sector, was now extended to include the area Zagazig-Mansourah-Damietta-Port Said (exclusive) and covered most of the two Provinces of Sharquia and Daqahlia, with a population of about 2 millions. The Brigade was now transferred from the control G.O.C. No.1 Section and became part of East Delta Force under the Command of Major-General Palin, commanding the 75th Division with Headquarters at Ismalia. While under General Palin's command our relations with him and his two Senior Staff Officers, Lt. Col. Dovey, D.S.O., and Lt. Col. Leaney, D.S.O., were of the most cordial and friendly nature.

My Command at the end of the month of March consisted of:

7th L.H. Regiment (Lt. Col. J. D. Richardson, D.S.O.) at Salhia

10th L.H. Regiment (Major L. C. Timperley) at Zagazig

11th L.H. Regiment (Lt. Col. P. J. Bailey, D.S.O.) at Mansourah

14th L.H. Regiment (Major A. S. Nobbs) at Abu Kebir

15th L.H. Regiment (Lt. Col. A. J. Mills) at Mit Ghamr

4 Machine Gun Squadrons, Armoured Cars, Trains & Boats.

My 8th (Lt. Col. T. J. Daly, D.S.O.) and 9th (Lt.Col. W. H. Scott, C.M.G., D.S.O.) Regiments were detailed for duty in adjoining Sectors.

On leaving Gen. Neale's command (No. 1 Section) I received a letter from him, complimenting the Australian Troops on the fine work they had done.

On the 3rd April the 11th Regiment arrived at Mansourah from Zagazig without having any trouble with the villagers en route. Mansourah is about 50 miles north of Zagazig and was the scene of the defeat of two great Crusades.

The first Egyptian Crusade in 1221, with a strength of 46,000 men, was marching from Damietta to Cairo. On arrival at Mansourah they were strongly opposed by the Egyptians. Everything was going well and the Egyptians were negotiating for the retirement of the Crusaders from Egypt in consideration of Jerusalem being handed back to the Christians. Just before negotiations were completed, however, the Nile rose in its annual flood, but much earlier than its usual time. The first the Crusaders knew about it was that their camps were under water and the horses were bogged. In those days the Canal system was not as efficient as at present. Now the Canals keep the floods in check, but in those days a large part of the Delta was inundated. The result of the flood was that the Crusaders could not move, and as the Egyptians held command of the Nile with their flotilla of galleys it ended up by the whole Christian Army surrendering.

The next disaster took place in the year 1250, when Louis, King of France, led the last Great Crusade. He landed at Damietta and moved towards Cairo, but was held up at Mansourah. In the battle that took place there the Christians rode through the Moslem Army, but carried their success so far that they became disorganised and the Mamelukes put up a stand. The Moslems then took charge of the Nile with their ships and prevented supplies coming up to Mansourah. All the dead bodies were thrown into the river, which had ceased to flow. A large amount of the food of the Crusaders consisted of eels, which subsisted on the diseased bodies in the river. Plague and sickness broke out in the Christian Army. After some months of these conditions the survivors of the Christian Army surrendered. A few were ransomed, many were killed, and the remainder were sold as slaves.

During the early part of the 11th Regiment's occupation of this district, demonstrations in the streets were made by the natives with the usual threats of what wonderful things they were going to do to the troops. In view of this a Mounted Troop was always kept as an inlying picquet ready for instant action. Shortly after the Regiment's arrival news was received at Regimental Headquarters that the natives were attacking a school, which was in the charge of an English lady teacher. The Troop at once galloped out to the scene. The natives were found rioting, smashing windows and pulling down fences with a view to burning down the buildings. The Officer in charge of the Troop, Major Lyons, D.S.O., dismounted the Troop and attacked the mob with the butt end of the rifles. He had previously given instructions that the bayonets were not to be used nor was the mob to be fired into without special orders. A few minutes of 'rough house' satisfied the rioters that they were not going to have their own way, and they promptly dispersed.

Patrols were now being sent out from all Regimental Headquarters, taking from one to three days on the tour. Where the railways had been destroyed the adjoining villagers were compelled to restore them, and where telegraph and telephone poles had been removed the same people were directed to bring them back. In all cases this was done without further trouble, word having apparently gone out that it was advisable to comply with these requests rather than be forced to do the work required.

On the 5th April a Squadron of the 11th Regiment stationed at Mansourah was sent to Damietta 40 miles from their Headquarters. This probably was the first time since the French were left in Egypt by Napoleon in 1801 that Foreign Troops had been seen in Damietta. The City is situated on the Damietta Branch of the Nile, and within a few miles of the Mediterranean Sea. As soon as the Squadron arrived they occupied some detached buildings and fortified their position so that in the event of their being attacked they could stand a siege. During the first few days there was a certain amount of trouble in this area - for the natives, who had never seen British Troops before. Several patrols were stoned, with the consequence that some of the natives were killed and others wounded. Where the Railway had been damaged it was restored by the natives.

From now on the reports of the patrols showed a cessation of hostility. From the middle of March to the 7th April, 1919, 343 villages in the Zagazig Sector were visited by Mounted Patrols. A large majority of the villagers had never seen European soldiers before, as the pre-war British Garrison was stationed in Cairo and never visited the Delta area.

General Allenby had now taken over the control of Egypt and given some concessions to the Nationalists. They, of course, thought they had won their independence and distributed leaflets graciously offering us safe conduct to our ships at Suez. We thought it would be a long time before we should ask for it. We, in our pride, thought a Light Horse Regiment could march from one end of the country to the other with absolute indifference to the wishes of the inhabitants.

At this time there were a number of Australian women in Cairo, consisting of Nursing Sisters, Canteen Workers, Officers' wives, etc. Australian Headquarters in Cairo, which had been almost denuded of troops, could not but feel responsible for the safety of these women, particularly as a large number of Egyptians in Cairo turned out and held street processions in open defiance of the Military Order forbidding it. It appeared to the Senior Australian Officers in Cairo that, should a rising occur there, lives might be lost before order was restored as no rallying point, where civilians could seek safety, had been arranged for. There was a small Australian Force guarding Turkish prisoners on Gazireh Island, situated on the Nile, in the heart of Cairo. There was also an Australian Military Hospital in the town with many inmates in the convalescent stage. Australian H.Q. arranged with these Hospital Authorities to form a Hospital Rest Camp on Gazireh Island, for some 300 convalescent men for whom arms were obtained, and this Force was organised as a defence rallying point and all British women in Cairo were quietly informed. A suggestion was made that these convalescents be sent away from Cairo on duty. Our H.Q. evaded this by inducing the Medical Authorities to refuse to discharge these men from Hospital supervision.

On the 12th April, I, with the Area Commander, Major General Palin, visited Salhia, where the 7th Regiment was stationed. This was the place where the 2nd Brigade started in April 1916 for the Sinai, and was Napoleon's starting point for his march to Acre in 1799. When we arrived we found the 7th in the throes of a Race Meeting, with a 'Tote' in full swing.

Provision for aerodromes at Zagazig and throughout the Sector was made, so that in the event of a breakdown of the Railways, communication by air could be carried out.

On the 30th April I was instructed to meet General Bulfin at the Railway Station at Zagazig, as the latter was passing through. General Bulfin, who had commanded the XXI Corps in the final operations in Palestine and Syria, now commanded all Troops in Egypt. He was very complimentary. He said he could not sufficiently express his appreciation of the work the Australians had done in this crisis, that they had been his one great standby, that they had done their work in a most soldierly manner and that he was proud to command them. It will be remembered that by the time the Rebellion had broken out in March apart from the Australian troops practically the whole of the British and Indian Units of Allenby's Army had been repatriated and there were then in Egypt only the small permanent garrison, the guards of the Prisoners of War Camps and a few details representing the British Army.

During the month of April a great deal had been done towards bringing the two Provinces comprising the Sector into a normal condition. Railways were repaired and a telegraph communication opened to Mit Ghamr and Mansourah. All Delta Light Railway Lines (except that from Mit Ghamr to Abu Hammad) were repaired under Australian supervision. The Railway lines to Mit Ghamr, Mansourah and Salhia were repaired entirely by us, assisted by natives from the adjoining villages. These railways had not been interfered with in any way since being repaired. Daily ration trains were being run to all these places. During the time the railway strike was in progress only one ration train (to Mansourah) failed to run, and this train missed only one day.

The town of Zagazig was maintained in a state of tranquility; so much so that though regarded by the British Authorities as a hot bed of Nationalism recourse was not had to fire-arms during the whole period of the trouble and two or three civilians only were wounded in the town with slight sword or bayonet wounds. The people of surrounding districts were quickly impressed by the mounted patrols, which were constantly moving through the country. At the end of April, except for the broken telegraph lines and the absence of ordinary passenger traffic on the railways, there was nothing to show there was any unrest in the country.

As evidence of the returning quietness in the Mansourah Sub-sector, which had longest remained truculent, we remarked that a large number of students were applying for passes to return to the schools at Cairo, Alexandria and Tanta, and the shops were remaining open all day at Mansourah.

That all was not peace and quietness it is recorded that at Salhia a native fired a revolver shot at a sentry but missed. The sentry returned the fire with similar results and the native got away in the darkness. Up to the end of April, 542 villages had been visited by the patrols.

In June a Sports Meeting and a Race Meeting were held at Zagazig and were very successful. One of the most spectacular events was the Chariot Race - four-in-hand with a half limber representing the Roman vehicle - driven from the limber.

On the 27th June Orders were issued for the 3rd L.H. Brigade to move from Zagazig to Moascar for embarkation to Australia and to hand over our posts to the 232nd and 234th Brigades.

During the month of June quiet had prevailed throughout the Sector. There was very little crime of any sort and no offence against Martial Law. No attempt was made during this month to interfere with either the railways or telegraphs. A few rumours of intended outrages on the railway in the Hehia Markaz were brought to the notice of these Headquarters but prompt steps taken prevented any overt act on the part of the malcontents. The Fast of Ramadan was celebrated and full liberty was given to the natives to carry out this great Mohammedan Festival with all ceremony.

On the 1st July General Allenby invited me to lunch at Cairo, when he expressed the highest admiration for the work the Australian Light Horse had done in the recent disturbances, for their efficiency, their thoroughness and their restraint.

On the 11th July the 3rd L.H. Brigade reimbarked for Australia.

P A R T   111

Thus ended our active service in the Great War. Apart from the fact that the "Originals" had been four and a half years away from Australia without any intervening visit to that place, our recent five months in Egypt had not been uninteresting. We had taken a very prominent part in the suppression of the rebellion. The weather conditions were ideal for campaigning, tents for all ranks were available, full army rations were issued, and extra food was procurable at reasonable rates. The work was not onerous and was interesting. Our casualties were very few. During the five months not more than half a dozen of our men were killed and only a few more wounded. The discipline was excellent. There was sufficient work to be done to keep the men from worrying about their repatriation. They were doing good work, they knew it and took a pride therein. Our relations with the British Authorities were most cordial. General Orders were received by us as to what was required of us, but no petty instructions were ever given as to how we were to carry them out.

The General Officers under whose control we were, General Allenby (High Commissioner), General Bulfin (G.O.C. Troops Egypt) and Major General Palin (East Delta Force) all expressed their satisfaction with the Australians. They had shown themselves during the War efficient and reliable Troops and the Authorities in Egypt treated them as such and allowed them to do their work without interference. The trust reposed in them was justified.

For the first week or so the position had been fraught with a certain amount of anxiety; we did not know exactly what we had to face. We knew we had the whole of the native population of Egypt against us but we did not know in what state of preparedness they were, what arms they had, and whether they had any army organisation. We, however, had the greatest confidence in ourselves, we had just come from Palestine and Syria where we had taken a prominent part in the greatest cavalry operations that the modern world had seen, such operations resulting in the complete annihilation of the enemy armies in that Theatre, armies consisting of the stout fighting Turks stiffened up with German troops. Our men were ideal for the work in front of them. Work for small patrols of mounted troops riding through country districts, far from supports, amongst a hostile population where the numbers were 100 to one against us, and where we could only succeed where we showed absolute indifference to the hostility of the local inhabitants. A patrol of one officer and twenty men would be sent out amongst the villages with instructions to go on a circuit of, say, 100 miles and return to Headquarters at the end of three days. These trips necessitated the frequent swimming of canals and a determined front to the hostile inhabitants with an absence of any trace of timidity. Hundreds of such patrols were sent out during our sojourn in this new Theatre, and in no single case did such patrol fail to uphold the traditions of the Australian Light Horse.

Instructions were issued that patrols sent into villages were to be strong enough to enforce their orders and in the event of trouble on no account was a withdrawal to be made. If help was required the patrol was to dig itself in and send for reinforcements. Not on one single occasion were these instructions disregarded and on no occasion could any of the natives say that they had chased or bluffed an Australian Patrol from its appointed route.

The fighting capacity of the natives was of a very low standard. Twentyfive centuries of continuous subjection to foreign rulers no doubt accounted for this. There are records of good fights put up by the Egyptian Armies in the Middle Ages, e.g. against the two Crusades at Mansourah in 1221 and 1250 previously referred to, and the defeat of the Mongols at Ain Jalud in the Plain of Esdraelon in 1260 when the Egyptian Army under Sultan Kutuz entirely destroyed the Mongol Army of 60,000 horsemen at that place. These results, however, were not brought about by Egyptian personnal but by the Mamalukes, professional all-time force of the Egyptian Sultans recruited from the children of foreigners captured in wars and brought up from childhood in the Moslem Faith as professional and regular soldiers. This magnificent body of troops, after being the mainstay of Egypt for six centuries, was destroyed by Sultan Mahomet Ali at the beginning of the last century, when, like most similar bodies of household troops, they had become too powerful for the safety of the Ruler.

As the natives apparently did not understand anything except force, what they required was some of the German frightfulness which our Teutonic friends exhibited towards the foreign civil populations under their control. We certainly never descended to these methods, but found it necessary to adopt stern measures to convince the natives that we intended to restore order. Like other Eastern races, including the Arabs in Palestine, they could not understand kindness or courtesy. If you treated them with those qualities they thought you were afraid of them and immediately adopted a truculent attitude. Cairo, the centre of British Administration, was the most turbulent part of the country. Orders were issued by Headquarters that the natives were not to be antagonised, that troops were to be confined to their quarters so as not to irritate the feelings of the natives, that the natives were to be allowed to have processions in the streets in support of their political claims, and to be allowed to fly such flags as they thought fit. The result was that any individual soldier that got away by himself into a side street was promptly murdered and insurgent mobs paraded the Cairo streets and displayed Turkish flags. There were, however, no processions or public meetings of rebels in our area and no rebel flags were aloft within the range of our vision.

As previously referred to in this Narrative, any physical opposition to our troops met with prompt punishment and in no single district had we to dispense such punishment twice. A single lesson was all that was required. As to confining our troops to their quarters, we adopted the opposite course and scoured the whole of our area with small but efficient patrols with results as before mentioned. The natives were given every opportunity and encouragement to return to their normal course of life. Those responsible for outrages were dealt with by the Military Courts, all of which were presided over by Australians and which Courts earned a name for fairness and justice.

In conclusion, with General Aspinall-Oglander in his "History of Gallipoli", I can, upon the termination of our war service, quote from Professor Smith's translation of "Aeschylus: Agamemnon" written twentyfive centuries ago, on the termination of a great war, the Siege of Troy 1182 B.C., as follows:-

"Aye, all's well, well ended. Yet, of what occurred in the long years, one might well say that part fell out happily, and part in turn amiss... For were I to recount our hardships and our wretched quarters, the scanted space and the sorry berths - what did we not have to complain of?.... Then again, ashore, there was still worse to loathe; for we had to lay us down close to the foeman's walls, and the drizzling from the sky and the dews from the meadows distilled upon us, working constant destruction to our clothes and filling our hair with vermin. And if one were to tell of the wintry cold, past all enduring, when Ida's snow slew the birds; or of the heat, what time upon his waveless noonday couch, windless the sea sank to sleep - but what need to bewail all this? Our labour's past .... What need for the living to count the number of the slain, what need to repine at fortune's frown? I hold it fitting that our misfortunes bid us a long farewell. For us, the remnant of the Argive host, the gain hath the advantage and the loss does not bear down the scale."

L. C. WILSON.

Brisbane,
9th March, 1934.

APPENDIX "A"

STANDING ORDERS - 3RD LIGHT HORSE BRIGADE

In view of the present state of unrest and lawlessness among the civil population, combined with their pretended friendliness with our troops, the following orders will come into force forthwith:-

(1) Troops are strictly forbidden to fraternise, or in any way mix with the civil population.

(2) All ranks will carry their arms when outside their bivouac areas, or billets, and on detached posts they will carry them whenever they leave their Headquarters.

(3) All ranks other than those on duty will remain in their quarters from 1830 till 0600, and be available for call at short notice.

(4) All Units, or detachments, will have an armed guard on duty during the night. Guard posts will be so sited that there will be no necessity for natives near them, and natives will not be allowed to come near the Headquarters of a post.

(5) Natives will not be allowed within the lines of Units, except those engaged for sanitary purposes.

(6) Alarm posts will be established for every Unit, or detachment. Practice "turn outs" will be carried out from time to time.

(7) After dark detachments, such as Orderlies, etc., will consist of at least two men.

(8) Except under exceptional circumstances, posts will not consist of less than 10 of all ranks.

(9) Mounted patrols will not consist of less than 4.

(10) Where a line of posts is guarding a railway, arrangements are to be made for frequent patrols between posts, at irregular intervals, even if no mounted men are available.

(11) Posts should arrange for defensive positions with the best local means at their disposal. On bombs being issued,

all posts and patrols will be provided with them. It is intended to issue flare pistols to posts. On issue of these a system of alarm signals will be arranged within the Unit.

(12) No Ghaffirs are to be allowed on the railway track between 7 p.m. and 5 a.m., but may be so employed by day. Subject to above any native found on the permanent way is to be shot at sight. Anyone found tampering with the railway by day or night, is to be shot. Movement between villages and towns between the hours of 7 p.m. and 5 a.m. is prohibited. Anyone contravening this will be arrested. Any native seen riding a cycle, motor cycle, or horse, is to be stopped and if not in possession of an authorised pass, is to be interrogated, and if not satisfactory, will be detained for further investigation.

(13) As the Brigade may be on its present duty some time, it is necessary that the matter of sanitation be thoroughly gone into. Each post will be provided with proper latrines and method of deposit of garbage.

(14) All ranks are warned against the danger of bilharzia, which may be contracted by merely washing in untreated water. Water is not safe unless either boiled, chlorinated, or filtered. C.O's. will see that detached posts are provided with means to chlorate.

Zagazig,
20/3/'19

L. C. WILSON
Brigadier General
Commanding 3rd Light Horse Brigade

APPENDIX "B"

DEFENCE SCHEME - ZAGAZIG SECTOR - 3rd Light Horse Brigade

APPRECIATION

(1) It is assumed for the purpose of this scheme that the inhabitants are doing their worst - that is - that the Egyptian Army, the Civil Police and the Civil Population are all in a state of insurrection.

(2) The troops under the command of this Sector are as follows:-

7th L.H. Regiment
10th L.H. Regiment
11th L.H. Regiment
14th L.H. Regiment
15th L.H. Regiment
1st M.G. Squadron
3rd M.G. Squadron (less 4 guns, 3 Officers)
2nd M.G. Squadron (less 64 other ranks)
1 Sub-section 4th A.M.G. Squadron
No. 2 Motor Launch
E.M.L. 7 (motor launch)
Armoured Car
Petrol Engine
Armed Motor Trolley

This does not include the troops guarding the P. of W. at Salhia, or those guarding the Officer P. of W. at Zagazig, which P. of W. camps are dealt with specially hereafter.

The factors to be considered when appreciating the situation are :-

The insurgents morale. This is of extreme low quality. They are absolutely wanting in personal bravery. They will not openly oppose troops, the most they are capable of doing is to make surprise attacks on small bodies, whom they expect to find off their guard. There is no possibility, therefore, of our troops in any number coming into armed conflict with them. Up to the present the insurgents have had practically no fire arms. If, however, the native soldiers and police join in, they will have a certain quantity. So far as the Provinces of Sharqia and Daqahlia are concerned, there are no Egyptian soldiers therein - they are not likely to be allowed to come here so we may dismiss them from our consideration. There remain the police and the village ghaffirs. Their rifles are practically all old pattern. Their ammunition is worse, consisting usually of slugs - their range would probably not exceed a hundred yards - rather too close for an Egyptian to fire at an armed soldier in daylight. No doubt they have a few modern rifles but at anything over a few hundred yards their markmanship would be of the poorest. I am quite satisfied therefore if we can keep our troops supplied with rations, forage and ammunition, the number of our troops in the Sector is sufficient to make the inhabitants behave themselves while there are any troops in their immediate neighbourhood, and that if they misbehave while the troops are actually absent, the troops are quite strong enough to punish them and deter them from so acting in future.

A general strike and passive resistance by all inhabitants of these Provinces would cause a certain amount of inconvenience, but would not have anything like such a general effect on the governing classes as would a general strike - say, in England. The country is rich in agricultural products and with our power of requisitioning, troops could live on indefinitely amongst the people, there would be practically no expenditure of ammunition and supplies would not cause much anxiety. It can be assumed that if a general insurrection was engineered the first insurgent action would be to pull up the railway and destroy the telephone and telegraph lines. Although they did not do it last time to any great extent, they could very easily destroy the roads so as to make them impassable for motor lorries, motor cars and motor cycles. In addition to digging ditches across them there are lots of places where they could flood them. There is one form of motor traction, however, that they could not defeat - motor caterpillar tractors. There are a large number of these vehicles at present at Kantara, and I am making application for some of them to be sent here.

It will, therefore, be seen that we may have to depend on horses for communication, (other than wireless and aeroplanes), by land, and on the canals for carriage of stores and rations.

The question of rations, however, should not be a serious one. If the whole of the inhabitants are hostile there should be no hesitation in requisitioning fully for food for man and horse. Thus there would only be a very small amount of such things as groceries, etc. to convey, which could be done weekly by barge or tractor.

In addition to the hostile action of the inhabitants, police, etc., the question of the P. of W. and civil prisoners is to be considered. I do not think, however, that these questions need cause much anxiety. The P. of W. camps have already got competent military guards. The civil prisoners are, I understand, confined in substantial buildings. As soon as the "Precautionary Period" commences, guards will be placed on these civil prisons to prevent the escape of the confinees.

PLAN

It is proposed to keep the Sector troops in the respective positions set out in the first part hereof. Those posts (other than the guards over the Zagazig-Salhia line), are all substantial bodies. They will form centres of resistance. They are quite strong enough to be able to protect themselves, they will form rallying points at which the non-Moslem inhabitants of the districts can concentrate, and be protected. These posts will be strong enough to send out patrols to collect the non-Moslem inhabitants when the occasion demands. The railway guards on the ZAGAZIG-SALHIA lines have, themselves, no reserves to reinforce that line if same is attacked at any point. To supply this defect the 7th L.H. Regiment will be responsible for supporting the line from SALHIA to AKIAD (inclusive). The 14th L.H. Regiment from AKIAD to HEHIA (inclusive), and the 10th L.H. Regiment from that last mentioned place to ZAGAZIG. These centres of resistance will also send out strong patrols to intimidate the villagers. Summary Courts could accompany these strong patrols and administer prompt justice in minor cases and where reprisals are authorised by higher authority, could take the necessary action on that behalf.

COMMUNICATIONS

The chief difficulty will be to keep in communication with the various units of the Sector. The usual methods, rail and wire, will, no doubt, go. Means available will be:

(a) <u>Wireless</u>. This will undoubtedly be the quickest and most satisfactory. There is at present a wireless set at ZAGAZIG and one at MANSOURAH. It is proposed to erect one at DAMIETTA. I strongly recommend that sets be erected at MIT GHAMR and if possible also at SALHIA AND ABU KEBIR. If there be a shortage of plants available, then in the above order, as, owing to the guards on the railways, it would be safe to send motor cyclists through to FAQUS. If the country were "up" it would not be safe to send cyclists from ZAGAZIG to MIT GHAMR or MANSOURAH, as the road runs through the centre of several large villages.

(b) <u>Aeroplanes</u>. At the present moment the communication by aeroplane is not satisfactory. Planes can, of course, drop messages, but at present cannot take them. We have at present no means of signalling to planes in the air. Our popham panels were handed in some time ago. There is at present at Zagazig no landing ground on which service machines will attempt to alight - there is a small ground on which light practice machines have landed, but I am informed that it is considered very dangerous. I understand that the air people are at present looking into the matter of forming a proper aerodrome here. I understand that a similar state of affairs exists at Mansourah, and that nothing whatever has been done at Mit Ghamr, Abu Kebir or Salhia. There should be no trouble whatever as regards the last mentioned place, as it is on the edge of the desert.

(c) D.R.L.S. I propose to be prepared to run a D.R.L.S. service by motor cycle from Zagazig to Faqus along the railway line and thence by mounted orderly to Salhia. This could be done with safety as there are a strong line of posts along that line at an average distance of 2 kilos. I am prepared to run a D.R.L.S. service from Zagazig to Mansourah with an escort of 12 all ranks. The 10th Regiment would supply the first relay to Diarb Negm, there it would be met at noon by a similar sized escort from Mit Ghamr and another from Simbillawein, there the escort would hand the D.R.L.S. over to a similar escort from Mansourah.

With regard to the communications of the posts at Faraskur, Damietta and Bosrat, these would be by sea via Port Said, as it is presumed that those places would be rationed from the last mentioned place.

(d) "Verey" pistols. With regard to the posts on the railway from Zagazig to Salhia it is proposed to equip each of these posts with a "Verey" pistol with the following system of signals:-

    WHITE illuminating or to draw attention.

    RED being attacked and required assistance.

    GREEN all clear, no assistance required.

RATIONS

All posts in the Sector are at present equipped with 7 days reserve and 3 days current. It is proposed to keep this reserve intact. As soon as the railway is cut, it is proposed to requisition forage for horses forthwith, and if practicable to get the men's rations by motor tractor or barge. If any undue delay by either of these methods - then requisition.

With regard to the different centres - Abu Kebir, Faqus and Salhia should continue to be rationed by rail from Zagazig as the whole line is guarded. If the rail by any chance was destroyed Abu Kebir could be rationed by road, so could Faqus. Salhia could be rationed from Kantara as previously, or by motor tractor.

Mit Ghamr and Mansourah could be rationed by the Mansourah canal from Benha. If motor tractors are made available both these places could be rationed, so far as men's rations are concerned, from Zagazig. The garrison at Simbillawein, (personnel), could be rationed from Zagazig by G.S. Wagon, or motor tractor. Faraskur, Damietta and Bosrat could be rationed from Port Said. The supplies being moved up from the wharves by train or wagon.

WATER

At present practically the whole of the personnel of the Sector are supplied with good water. In the big towns this is supplied through the Municipality. It is quite possible that if there were a general strike this source of supply would cease. There is ample canal water through the whole Sector, and if the worst comes to the worst, this water could be used after boiling. Apparently chlorination is not sufficient to kill bilharzosis.

NON-MOSLEM INHABITANTS

Permanent post O's.C. have been ordered to ascertain the number of these persons in their respective areas and to reconnoitre suitable camps for same, taking into consideration (a) safety of camp, and (b) convenience for rations and for evacuation.

PRECAUTIONARY MEASURES TO BE TAKEN AT ONCE

All O's.C. permanent posts have been instructed to place them in an all round state of defence, both to protect themselves from being rushed and to protect themselves against possible rifle fire, and to place therein the prescribed reserve of rations and ammunition for garrison, and to make proper provision for protection of rations for refugees, and petrol for works of public utility. As above stated, they have been instructed to ascertain numbers of non-Moslems and reconnoitre site for refugees camp.

PRECAUTIONARY METHODS TO BE TAKEN UPON RECEIVING NOTIFICATION THAT THE "P.P." HAS COMMENCED

Make certain that all essential guards (water supplies, electric light plant, etc.) are sufficiently strong. Warn necessary civilians of rendezvous arranged for them. Put guards on civil prisons.

MEASURES TO BE TAKEN IN THE EVENT OF AN ACTUAL RISING

Collect refugees, requisition food for same, if not already in hand. Patrol vigorously. Reinstitute restrictions on movement, i.e. - Prohibit movement between towns and villages between 1900 and 0500, and keep all inhabitants of towns in their houses between the same hours. Prohibit processions and meetings exceeding 10 in number.

P. OF W. CAMPS

Special arrangements will be made with regard to the outside guarding of the prisoners of war at Zagazig and Salhia after conference with the C.O. of the P. of W. guard.

REPORT ON REPAIRING RAILWAY BETWEEN ZAGAZIG AND MANSOURAH AND ABU KEBIR AND FAQUS - Reference map Faqûs 1/100,000

Under instructions from 3rd L.H. Brigade Headquarters, I left Zagazig on the morning of 29th March, 1919, in charge of a party to repair the railway between Zagazig and Salhia. The party consisted as follows:-

1. One mounted troop from the 9th L.H. Regt., Lieut. Wagg in charge, to leave Zagazig at 0700.

2. A construction train with a party of about 60 Egyptian platelayers. There was no European in charge of this party. A guard of 9 men in charge of Cpl. Maddern was attached to the train. The train to leave Zagazig at 0800.

3. One motor lorry with 12 men and a Hotchkiss rifle to leave at 0800.

Mr. Nicholson was attached to the mounted troop and Mr. Cranston to the motor lorry.

The first and third party met about 0845 at the first break in the line at Rafr El Mesallamia. The break at this point was five sections of rails. One section had the rails removed from the sleepers and the whole thrown in the canal. The other four sections had been undone at the fishplates and tipped intact into the canal. All material was recovered. The mounted troop with Mr. Nicholson went into the village and collected about 300 natives to replace the material on the railroad. In the meanwhile the motor lorry party had collected about 100 other volunteers. Great care was taken to see that we had no civil servants or others that Messrs. Nicholson and Cranston thought should not be put to work. A certain proportion informed us that they had never worked and most of these gentlemen had flash boots and socks. As far as possible they and other sulky parties went into the canal to do the dirty work and the fellahin pulled on the ropes on dry land. In most cases the supply of the former was not sufficient for the job, so the fellahin made up the required number in the canal. The fellahin right through looked upon it as a big joke and gave no trouble at all once we had them, but the other class was decidedly annoyed because he thought his dignity was upset. The second break was about one mile on the Zagazig side of El Edwa. Before the first break had been completed Lt. Wagg and Mr. Nicholson had taken the mounted troop on to Edwa to get a further party of volunteers to repair the second break.

To make sure that we would not be delayed on account of labour troubles I marched the volunteers from the first break up to the second. The Kafr el Mesallamia party of workers thought it very hard that they should have to mend the Edwa break for they were very particular to impress on me that they were a good village and had broken nothing and that Edwa was a very bad village.

The Edwa people had the same story and so on through every village. In fact, the line wreckers must have come from a considerable distance, quite outside the radius of Mr. Wagg and his mounted troops. This theory was slightly upset by the local swimming parades, for as the water was cold they lost no time in looking for sleepers, etc., where they were not, but went straight to where they were. The second break was a bad one, consisting of about 12 sections of rails. In every case only the fishplates had been unbolted and the sections were tipped into the canal in one lift. The wrecking party must have been at least 200 men. On the arrival of the reinforcements from Edwa we had a very satisfactory working party. With about 100 in the canal and about 300 on the ropes we pulled the sections out in no time. The Omdah from Edwa came along with his party and was of the greatest assistance in working the gangs. This section of the break was not complete before dark, so we let the volunteers go for the night. We gave instructions to the Omdah of Edwa to produce 200 volunteers at 0530. This he promised to do. The next morning he arrived with them about an hour late for parade.

I learned later that he had had considerable trouble in his village collecting his men, and was threatened with violence. However, he got them out and brought them along and up to the time we had finished he was again of the greatest assistance in directing his men.

In the meanwhile Lt. Wagg and Mr. Nicholson had gone out with the mounted troop for further hands west of the railway. After proceeding a short distance a white flag appeared out of a ditch. Mr. Nicholson rode over to the flag and a man appeared, to whom he explained what he wanted. The owner of the flag called out at the top of his voice and from all crops, adjacent ditches and holes, heads of very scared men appeared and gradually came in, and on hearing what was wanted and they had every prospect of seeing another sunrise, came along a very orderly crowd. This party, with the Edwa workers, gave us a very good working party, and we quickly found all the material in the canal and finished this break and got on to the next and biggest break about half a mile beyond Hehia.

Word had been sent on to Hehia for a strong working party to be on their break in the railway. Lt. Wagg and Mr. Nicholson, with a mounted troop, went ahead of the train to Hehia and found that no notice had been taken of the instructions.

Mr. Nicholson sent for the Omdah and the Namour Markaz but in each case an evasive answer was sent. A one star lieut. of police with red hair was in attendance and with the aid of Mr. Wagg got together about 100 workers, and proceeded to the break. The workers naturally adopted the attitude of the Omdah, and were a very sulky and unsatisfactory lot of volunteers. Mr. Nicholson and Crampton went

back to Zagazig during the afternoon after leaving word for
the Omdah and the Namour Markaz to have 250 men ready early in
the morning. This break was only about half finished by the
evening, so we camped for the second night near the break.
The train did not return to Zagazig this evening like it had
done the previous one. In the morning no volunteers appear-
ing, Mr. Wagg and myself with a mounted troop went into the
village to enquire into the reason. We found the red-headed
police officer had collected about 50, but was unable to get
them to move out to the break. With the aid of our mounted
men the police officer quickly got the required number. This,
however, had caused a serious delay. I sent for the Omdah,
but again he did not turn up. We got our party along to the
break and got them to work, but here a lot of sleepers were
missing and could not be found. They were not in the canal,
as a very extensive swimming parade was carried out all the
morning and up to the time we had finished the break. We had
no lack of material for this parade for the workers had a very
big per cent of sulky members and they all went in. Some were
so sulky they would not undress, but eventually they were per-
suaded to go in clothes and all. Mr. Nicholson had arrived
before this, Mr. Crampton having stayed behind in Zagazig, and
he advised me who should swim and who shouldn't, for many of
them had such beautiful boots I was a bit nervous myself of
wetting them.

When everything was working smoothly Mr. Nicholson and
myself went back to enquire into the absence and lack of help
of the Omdah and the Namour Markaz. Again we drew a blank,
for the two gentlemen refused to produce themselves, I would
like to draw the attention of the authorities to these two
gentlemen, for up till the present they must be of the opinion that they have had a win. No attempt was made either to
produce or account for the missing material.

Midway between Hehia and Abu Kebir there was another
break of about 7 sections. Beyond the fact that many sleepers were missing and could not be found nothing out of the
common occurred. Next break was about 1 mile before we
reached Abu Kebir. Here we found a very good working party
waiting and who had already picked out the material from the
canal and cleared the railbed. I had arranged with Lieut.
Wagg to send a section on early in the morning to Lieut.
MacGregor, asking him to arrange for this working party, and
he had done it very well. A lot of sleepers were missing at
this break and there was no attempt to produce them or explain
their absence. This break used up most of the spare material

the repair train was carrying, so the train returned to Zagazig and returned just at dark with extra material, also rations for the 14th Regiment.

This completed all the breaks up to Abu Kebir and we camped that night near the 14th Regiment. I had seen General Wilson during the repair of this line and he had ordered me to proceed along the Mansourah line and repair that first. Starting from Abu Kebir the next morning I left the motor lorry and Mr. Wagg and his troop behind, for I was told that the breaks were so far apart that the mounted troops would never catch up.

The road on from Abu Kebir is impossible for a motor lorry, the first break being about a mile from Abu Kebir. The local police arranged for this working party, and as only two sections were up we quickly repaired this and pushed on. A number of sleepers were missing. To-day for the first time the Egyptian State Railway gang worked with a will, for they were running short of rations. Before they had always been willing enough, but if there was a wrong way of doing a job they would adopt it. Taking it all in all they were the most uneconomical and stupid lot of workers I have ever met.

After mending this break we had a good run to Kafr Saqr, where we were informed there was only one break between there and Mansourah. This break was found on the bridge which crosses the canal near Abu El Shegig. Here we found a repair train from Mansourah repairing this break. The train from Mansourah had found no break as we had expected. The bridge was damaged slightly, but in no vital way. As there was only 1 section of rails missing we left the Mansourah truck to repair this and returned to Abu Kebir, as I was anxious to push on to repair the line to Faqus.

On arriving at Abu Kebir I found that Lieut. Wagg had been ordered to return to Zagazig by the C.O. of the 14th Regiment. The C.O. 14th Regiment told me that there were only two breaks between Abu Kebir and Faqus and none after, except the bridge to Salhia, and that he had arranged for working parties at these two breaks. After Faqus to Salhia he informed me there was a bridge about 3 miles from Faqus which was down, otherwise there was no break. This being the case, he had ordered Lieut. Wagg home, as the 14th would do his work. From hereon Lieut. Wagg and his troop were greatly missed, for the 14th Regiment did not have the parties ready and not till I had walked back to the 14th

Headquarters and got them to send out and get working parties for me could I get on with the job. Lieut. Wagg up to this had never kept the repair party waiting one minute.

The first break on the Faqus line was only about 250 yards from 14th Regiment's Headquarters. Lieut. MacGregor took charge and repaired this break, while I marched about 100 natives up to the next break. Here I found a section of the 14th Regiment guarding the break. With the men I had brought up the work on this break was started till the 14th Regiment's section had secured more workers. By the time the break had been repaired it was too late to push on to Faqus, so we returned to Abu Kebir and camped where we had the previous night. The C.O. 14th Regiment told me here that a railway strike was expected the next day, so in case of trouble we were ready with an emergency crew for the train. I was sure there would be no trouble with the E.S.R. gang that they had, for they were too slow to ever catch up a rumour. The C.O. 14th Regiment this night arranged with the Omdah of Abu Kebir for rations for the 60 natives of the repair train for 24 hours.

Next morning we ran through to Faqus without a break. Here the 14th Regiment arranged for a working party of 200 men to proceed to the bridge which was broken. Two sections of the rails were missing Faqus side of the canal, and one on the other. We repaired the line up to the canal so the steam crane could operate and came back to Faqus, where we found the train with the steam crane had arrived. This train had two Europeans in charge. They went to the bridge and examined the damage and annexed what part of my repair train and natives they required, and informed me that my services were no longer required. I arrived at Zagazig at 1900, the bridge ought to be repaired in about 10 hours.

GENERAL IMPRESSIONS

The impression that I gathered repairing these lines is that the whole district is thoroughly cowed and that they will not damage anything further while there are any troops about.

The whole of this repair job was carried out without bloodshed, and as soon as the fellahin found out he was not going to be hurt he treated it as a huge joke and thoroughly enjoyed seeing the next in the social scale going into the canal. The higher the social scale the more his dignity was hurt and the more the fellahin enjoyed it. In one case £25 was offered to the men to let an extra flash gentleman off. I am afraid he went in, overcoat and all. One could not help observing that the better dressed and more educated were, if possible, greater cowards than the fellahin.

One of Lieut. Wagg's troopers who was about 1 mile west of the railway on the canal west from Kafr El Messalimia reported to Lieut. Wagg that he was fired on from one of the crops. There was no village near and he was unable to locate where the shot came from.

I would like to thank Messrs. Nicholson and Cranston for their untiring help. Mr. Nicholson was with the party up to the time Lieut. Wagg and his troop returned from Abu Kebir. Without his help and knowledge of local conditions the operation could not have been carried out at such an early date.

(Sgd.) A. U. MARTIN, Lieut.
10th L.H. Regiment.

ZAGAZIG, 3/4/'19

www.ingramcontent.com/pod-product-compliance
Lightning Source LLC
Chambersburg PA
CBHW070935160426
43193CB00011B/1690